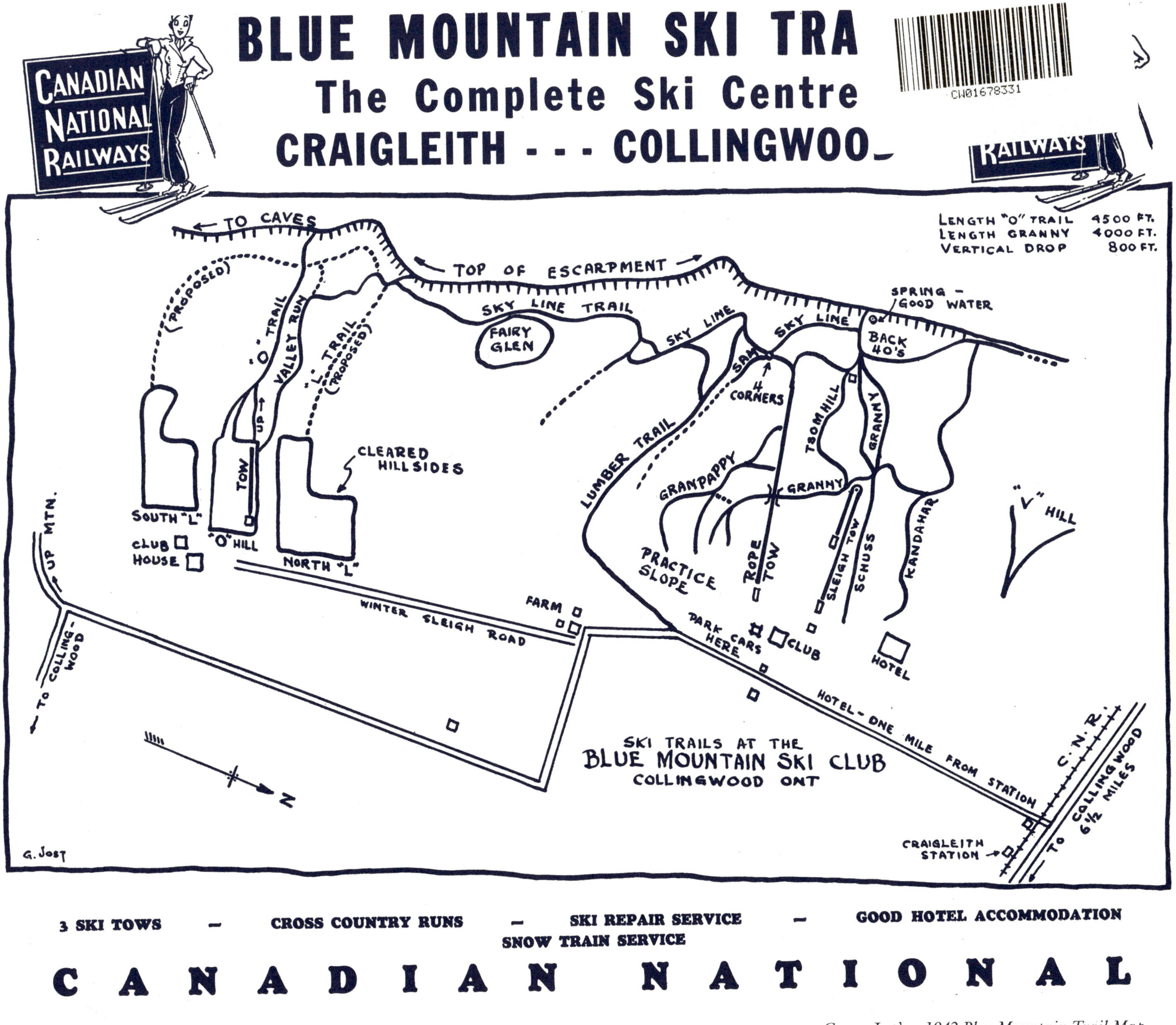

George Jost's c. 1942 Blue Mountain Trail Map.
– Courtesy: Paul Hughes, Credit: George Jost

BLUE
MOUNTAIN

BLUE MOUNTAIN

GEORGE WEIDER

THE BOSTON MILLS PRESS

Canadian Cataloguing in Publication Data

Weider, George
Blue Mountain

Includes bibliographical references and index.
ISBN 1-55046-009-9

1. Weider, Jozo. 2. Blue Mountain Resorts Limited – History. 3. Ski resorts – Ontario – Blue Mountain Region – History. 4. Skis and skiing – Ontario – Blue Mountain Region – History. I. Title.

GV854.8.C3W44 1990 338.7'6179693'0971318
C90-095738-7

Published by:
THE BOSTON MILLS PRESS
132 Main Street
Erin, Ontario N0B 1T0
(519) 833-2407
Fax: (519) 833-2195

American Association for State and Local History Award of Merit

Winners of the Heritage Canada Communications Award

Design by Gillian Stead
Edited by Noel Hudson
Typography by Lexigraf, Tottenham
Printed by Tri-Graphic, Ottawa

The publisher wishes to acknowledge the financial assistance and encouragement of The Canada Council, the Ontario Arts Council and the Office of the Secretary of State.

To Barbara

Contents

Preface

I started research for this book several years ago, but the publication has been timed to coincide with the celebration of the 50th anniversary of the founding of Blue Mountain Resorts Limited in 1941. In the 50 years of its existence the resort acquired hundreds of loyal patrons, many of whom became friends of our family. A number of these skiers and several local residents have been very generous in helping me with this project. I would like to express my thanks to all who contributed. My indebtedness is particularly great to those who trusted me by providing their cherished scrapbooks and mementos for my perusal.

Major inspiration for the project came from three dynamic women, each of whom has made her mark on the Blue Mountain area. They knew the story was in me and urged me to get on with it when I was hampered by health problems and business demands. Shiela Metras of the Georgian Triangle Tourist Association and Bev Philp, Vice-President of Marketing at Blue Mountain, encouraged me in every phase of the project, read my manuscript, and made valuable suggestions. My wife, Barbara, has been a trusted editor of everything that I have written, including a bulky PhD dissertation in Russian history. The present work was improved by her review.

My sister Helen McGillivray corroborated much of my information on our life at the resort and provided her well-kept scrapbooks. My mother, also named Helen, gave me some good ideas on what to write about and filled in some gaps in my knowledge of our family history. I am also grateful to my brother-in-law Gordon Canning, President of Blue Mountain. His keen sense of humour and ability to remember anecdotes have enlivened some of the subject matter from the 1970s and 1980s.

While this historical sketch mainly focuses on the activities of Jozo Weider and Blue Mountain Resorts, it is rounded out by a brief outline of the development of the neighbouring private ski clubs. This was done primarily with the help of Wendy Ward-Price of Osler Bluff, Doug Bowie and Gord Cummings of Craigleith, Philip Durnford and Hans Kent of Alpine, Ian Rogers of Georgian Peaks, and Michael Gee and Mr. and Mrs. T.B. Lailey of Devil's Glen. Allison Kingsmill generously allowed me to read and use material from an unpublished manuscript on the early history of Osler Bluff. Equally indispensable were Molly Main's *History of Craigleith Ski Club* and an outline of the history of the Devil's Glen Country Club, prepared by Diane Crews. Peter Kingsmill was a mine of information about both the formation of the Osler Bluff club and the early years at Blue Mountain. Numerous other private club members were also consulted.

John Robert Colombo provided important advice on shaping the format of the book and directed me to a publisher. Another friend, Marc Egnal of the York University History Department, read the manuscript and helped me with style and organization. Further improvements were made by editor Noel Hudson. Frank McNulty, President of the Toronto Ski Club, kindly made available a valuable collection of club records and minutes, as well as back issues of the club's newsletter, *The Ski-Runner*. The same type of help was rendered by Ken Miller, Past President of the Collingwood Ski Club. Three former Toronto Ski Club presidents, Ross Wilson, Ross Larway and Bob Gooch, provided very knowledgable advice on the role of the TSC in the origins of ski resort development at Blue Mountain. Generous assistance was provided by Bill Tindale, President of the Canadian Ski Museum, and by Ted McDonald, Honorary Assistant Curator. Ed Champagne of the National Alpine Ski Team was very efficient in supplying photographs and information about World Cup racers. Tracy Marsh, Curator of the Collingwood Museum, contributed photographs and documents compiled for the museum's 1988 exhibit on local ski history. Mayor Joe Sheffer and the Town of Collingwood gave me permission to incorporate parts of a memoir that I contributed to the town's historical anthology, *Reflections*, in 1983. Former Collingwood Township Clerk-Treasurer Bill Knott was very obliging in reviewing records of the township's liquor plebiscites.

Jack MacMurchy of the *Stayner Sun* was a long-time observer of the ski scene while involved in the Blue Mountain Ski Club and in newspaper publishing in Collingwood. He qualified as patroller no. 79 in the Canadian Ski Patrol System and headed the Collingwood patrol in 1948. For several decades he was a tireless skiing promoter and organizer in the town. His writings and collection of photographs were crucial to the book. Additional help came from George Czerny, the irrepressibly cheerful editor of the *Enterprise-Bulletin* and a valued friend. Sue Boehm provided a wonderful collection of photos taken by her late father, Les Tucker, in the 1940s. Barbara Kemp was very helpful in supplying material about her husband, Robert, the Artist's Studio and the surrounding chalets. Mrs. Walter Trier and her daughter, Gretl Fodor, gave permission to include Trier paintings and helped me with the selection. I have utilized information on Craigleith provided by John Goodchild, Donald

Plater, Marcella Keith, and local historian and archaeologist Charles Garrad. Charlie's knowledge of the subject is impressive and was heavily relied upon. Fritz Schuller was most co-operative in allowing me to use several of his fine photographs. His successor at Schuller Fotography, Steve Montgomery, was also very helpful with photographic services.

My biggest debt is to Marijane Thomas. After serving many years at Blue Mountain, initially as Blue Mountain's first full-time ski patroller, she had just taken a leave of absence, and it was my good fortune that she was available from September 1989 to be my assistant. I first assumed that she would primarily be a typist and researcher, but she turned into a trusted collaborator, without whom this project would not have seen publication. With her enthusiastic interest in the people and events at Blue Mountain, she was a relentless hunter of photographs, which she meticulously organized in relation to the text. While Marijane and I have gone to great lengths to verify dates of photographs and the names of people in them, primarily by cross-examining witnesses, there may well be disputes and mistakes, as in many cases decades have elapsed since the photos were taken. I apologize for any errors that may be found in the captions and text, and emphasize that I am solely responsible for all the material presented in this book.

George Weider
Blue Mountain, September 1990

Foreword

The Blue Mountain area took on a new significance for me in 1957. I met Nancy Fisk, a Collingwood native, and she changed my life in many ways. She revealed to me the special nature of the Collingwood-Blue Mountain area and became my wife in 1960.

I had never been on a pair of skis in my life. I had been a hockey and lacrosse player in my younger days, but had no interest in skiing whatsoever. All of that changed when Nancy took me out to Blue Mountain in December 1957. On borrowed equipment (some of it her hand-me-downs) I found a new meaning for the terms "rope tow" and "Apple Bowl." I learned that getting up the hill was, for a novice, more difficult than coming down the hill.

Since my first run down Blue Mountain on that December day more than three decades ago, I have been enamoured with skiing. It is the only sport I know in which a novice can enjoy the same excitement and have as much fun as an expert. I have skied in all parts of the USA, Canada and Europe, and I still love to come back to Blue Mountain.

Our children, Allen and Jill, now grown up, learned to ski at Blue Mountain. They soon surpassed their parents in ability and now barely tolerate our presence on hills with them. We joined Georgian Peaks Ski Club in the Sixties and Craigleith Ski Club in the Seventies. We have spent every winter since the late Fifties on or near Blue Mountain.

My friendship with the Weider family began with the late Jozo Weider. I shared many airplane trips to and from Nassau with him in the 1960s, and he told me of his dreams for Blue Mountain. He wanted Blue Mountain to become a destination ski area rather than a day-visitor ski area. The Weider family has made Jozo's dream come true.

My wife, Nancy, went to Collingwood District Collegiate Institute. One of her classmates was George Weider, Jozo's only son. George and I became friends in the 1970s because of our mutual interest in the Soviet Union. George and his wife, Barbara, studied in Moscow, and we have shared some wonderful evenings and stories.

George is in a unique position to tell the story about Blue Mountain. He grew up at the resort and helped his father in the pioneering stages of the resort and pottery businesses. He was an observant witness and records many interesting incidents from the first 50 years. He has been trained as a professional historian and has interviewed dozens of skiers and employees about their experiences. Also, he has ranged beyond Blue Mountain to describe the private clubs that grew up on both sides of the resort: a phenomenon unique to Ontario. He describes the coaching programs and the emergence of international skiing stars from Blue Mountain and the private clubs. People who visit Blue Mountain from Europe find it hard to believe that such a small "mountain" could possibly have been the training area for so many World Cup racers.

The Weider family has taken great risks and made a huge commitment in expanding the operation that they inherited from Jozo. They are fortunate to have a strong business leader in Gordon Canning, for whom I have great respect. His vision for Blue Mountain is similar to the vision that Jozo had for it.

My family members all enjoy Blue Mountain. It is part of our life. George Weider, in this book, has let us share his family's knowledge and his family's dream.

R. Alan Eagleson
September 1990

El Cousens of the Toronto Ski Club making a jump turn, c. 1930. – Courtesy: Canadian Ski Museum

PART I

Blue Mountain Before Jozo

Four hundred and fifty million years ago, what is now the Blue Mountain area lay under a warm, shallow sea. The sea withdrew, leaving a height of land like the rim of a saucer. Some reshaping came about as a result of glacial action; the face of the escarpment was eroded and weathered by the Pleistocene glaciers in the last one to two million years. Commanding the greatest vertical drop in Southern Ontario – the highest point on the escarpment is on Osler Bluff at 1,770 feet above sea level – Blue Mountain was perfectly located to become the major ski destination for the heavily populated urban centres of the province.

It took a great many pioneering efforts, however, for this to come about. The Toronto and Blue Mountain ski clubs must be given credit for their initiative and ingenuity in discovering the ski area and launching its initial development. And even after Blue Mountain became a commercial resort, the clubs continued to provide a focus for families and a social nucleus for the resort and the community. They were also a primary force in the organization and promotion of competitive events and training programs. Many of Canada's best racers got their start this way.

When the Blue Mountain Ski Club was putting the first tows on the mountain in the late 1930s, Jozo Weider, the man who was eventually to found the company that would make the resort a thriving commercial operation, was encamped in a remote chalet in the Carpathian Mountains. The political upheavals in Europe brought him to Canada as an immigrant in 1939, and he arrived at Blue Mountain to start his work in 1941.

The Toronto Ski Club

Toronto led the way in organizing skiers. The Toronto Ski Club (TSC) was formed in 1924. It grew quickly and by 1940 was the largest local ski club in the world, with 7,000 skiers. Home base was at Summit, on the northern edge of Toronto, but the club also developed operations at Dagmar, Caledon and Blue Mountain. The club had very genteel origins. A fox-hunting trumpet was used to call skiers to the slopes, and skiing technique was developed from books written by English gentlemen who had skied in Switzerland. However, the club was far from being a preserve of the wealthy. In 1940, annual fees were only $3.75 for "Men's Senior," $1 for "Junior," and a skier could be completely outfitted with clothing and equipment for less than $25.

During the 1930s and 1940s the TSC provided technical or financial assistance to virtually every club in Southern Ontario, including Blue Mountain. This led to equity ownership in the Blue Mountain resort that lasted until 1986, when its eight-percent holding was purchased by the Weider group. Toronto Ski Club stalwarts Sam Cliff, Fred Hall, Ross Larway, Ross Wilson and Tom McGoey were pioneers of the Blue Mountain ski area, along with the Collingwooders led by John Smart and Norman Boadway. The early Toronto group was followed by capable successors such as Victor Blackhall, Bob Gooch and Michael Davies. Under their guidance the club developed the strong racing program that ultimately produced National Team skiers Kellie Casey, Liisa Savijarvi and the inimitable Todd Brooker.

The early club leaders were dynamic and entrepreneurial, acting as missionaries to towns near ski hills. They drove up to Collingwood or Flesherton through snowstorms, and they recruited new skiers by showing ski movies and demonstrating new techniques and equipment. The Toronto skiers enjoyed themselves immensely on ski trains to Quebec, Huntsville and Blue Mountain, and sometimes took longer trips to Banff and other parts of the Rockies. They did much volunteer work cutting trails and organizing competitions. This was a congenial and high-minded set of young sportsmen and sportswomen. When war broke out, the armed services made use of their patriotism and leadership skills.

The Toronto Ski Club had many war heroes, at least two of whom deserve mention. Bomber pilot Julian Sale lost his life in the war after winning the Distinguished Flying Cross and the Distinguished Service Order. He had been extremely popular in skiing circles, and the Julian Sale award was established by the club in his memory. Ross Wilson, who was an Olympic ski jumper and who took part in numerous international Nordic competitions in the 1930s, had a remarkable navy career and was lucky to survive the war. Wilson was one of the chief instigators of the TSC's involvement in the Collingwood operation and later participated in the founding of two ski resorts. When the war ended he put his uniform away and resumed skiing. In 1947, with Tom McGoey, Fred Foy and Sport Hambly, he founded the Happy Valley ski resort, a short-lived venture that was later absorbed by Blue Mountain. It was a miracle that

Toronto Ski Club members at Summit, c. 1933. Left to right: Bob Reynolds Jr., Bob Reynolds, Mrs. Vanstone, Mary Larway, Frank Vanstone, Ross Larway and Harry Lackie. – Courtesy: Ross Larway

Blue Mountain before there were tows, c. 1936. – Courtesy: Collingwood Museum

Ross Wilson as a young lieutenant on HMS Dorchester, *the Royal Navy cruiser that finished off the German battleship* Bismarck *in a great sea battle in the Atlantic. In 1942 the* Dorchester, *with Wilson aboard, was blown apart and sunk by Japanese dive bombers in the Indian Ocean. While floating with his life-preserver, he was strafed by Japanese planes, but he survived and was picked up after 32 hours in the water. A year later, while serving on another vessel, he was sunk again, this time by German bombs in the Mediterranean. He finished the war as a corvette captain in the Royal Canadian Navy, with the rank of lieutenant-commander.*
– Courtesy: Ross Wilson

Ross Wilson with teammates at the 1932 Olympics at Lake Placid, New York. Left to right: Sigurd Lockeberg (Manager), Louis Grimes (Coach), Jostein Nordmoe, Art Gravel, Karre Engstad, John Currie, Bud Clark, Nip Stone, Bob Lymburne, Howard Bagguley, Hubert Douglas, John P. Taylor, Ross Wilson, Jacques Landry and Norm Gagné. Absent: Harry Pangman and Walter Ryan.
– Courtesy: Canadian Ski Museum

Ross lived to be feted at age 80 in a celebration staged at Georgian Peaks in March 1990. As well as some harrowing war experiences, he had suffered terrible injuries when he skied off a cliff near his old Happy Valley resort.

The Blue Mountain Ski Club

The first skiers to make use of Blue Mountain were local enthusiasts who climbed and skied the hills on the Carmichael, Doherty and Goodchild farms in the mid-1930s. In 1935 they formed the Blue Mountain Ski Club at a meeting chaired by John Smart, the dynamic and successful owner of a canning factory in Collingwood. In that first season (1935-36) the club rented a room in the back of Andrew Goodchild's farmhouse for $40 and used it as a clubhouse. In 1938 the club acquired the neighbouring 150-acre Doherty farm for $1,200 after leasing it the previous season. The centre of activities was a log cabin that had been part of the original Doherty homestead.

The early skiers had to be very hardy, especially in the first few years of the club. That era is vividly remembered by Bert Brydon, who established an electrical business in Collingwood in 1932 and went from house to house repairing radios at 50 cents a call. Brydon took up skiing around 1935, the year in which the new ski club was formed, and he helped build some of the early tows on the mountain. "There were a few trails at the north end that had been cut by the Doherty brothers," he recalls, "but you were taking your life in your hands to ski on them. You cannot imagine how dangerous the conditions were. There were stumps and rocks sticking up all over the place. I went schussing down one trail and all of a sudden there was nothing underneath my skis but air." Brydon suffered a fearsome crash into a ravine that had simply been left in the middle of a trail. He hung up his skis and never set foot on the hill again. "I couldn't afford to get hurt; my business was a one-man show," he explains. Other veterans of the era speak of trails that suddenly ended in the middle of a forest, sending unwary skiers into the trees if they failed to brake to a stop in time.

The trails above the log cabin were improved by Fritz Loosli, a Swiss instructor engaged by the Toronto and Blue Mountain clubs between 1936 and 1939. He spent some time at Summit, but most of his work was at Blue Mountain. Loosli was paid a salary of $200 by the Toronto Ski Club in 1937. The following year, in return for 10 days of Loosli's services and $50 in cash, the Toronto Ski Club received skiing privileges from the Blue Mountain Ski Club. It does not appear that Loosli's lessons were very elaborate; his advice on how to run the gully on the Granny was, "Start whistling while at the top and keep whistling until you're safely down."

In December 1936 Loosli informed the Collingwood *Enterprise-Bulletin*: "For over a month I have had 10 men cutting trails and down-

Competitors in Blue Mountain Ski Club's meet, January 1955. Left to right: Don Scouler, R. Miller, J. Smith (winner), and R. Hunter.
– Courtesy: Jack MacMurchy, Credit: Herb Hall

Toronto ski pioneer Ross Larway in 1937. He played a key role in the Toronto Ski Club's involvement with the Blue Mountain Ski Club. – Courtesy: Ross Larway

The Swiss professional Fritz Loosli played a key role in the origins of the ski operation at Blue Mountain between 1936 and 1939. In the 1940s he taught skiing in Quebec and was technical advisor to the Peterborough Ski and Toboggan Company. – Courtesy: Toronto Ski Club

hill runs for beginners, third, second and first class skiers. The downhill runs have a vertical drop of 750 feet and vary in length from two-thirds of a mile to a mile and a half." These trails, the Granny, Schuss and Kandahar, were to remain the principal runs at the north end of the resort throughout the decades that followed. Many of the trail-cutters of the Thirties were unemployed workers assigned to the job by the Town of Collingwood, which administered a relief program for those in need. Logs from the trails were brought into Collingwood and sold for firewood.

In 1940 the Toronto Ski Club and the Blue Mountain Ski Club joined forces to improve the ski facilities. The co-operative effort is remembered by Ross Larway, who was active in the Toronto club at the time. He was an avid skier and a partner in a sports equipment company which sold waxes and boot dubbins and imported Gresvig skis from Norway. Larway, Temple and Cooper were among the first of the ski merchants to install steel edges when the customer required them. As Secretary-Treasurer of the Canadian Amateur Ski Association in 1936, Larway was a leading organizer, together with President Fred Hall, of the first Dominion Championships to be held in Ontario; they took place in Toronto and Flesherton in 1936. The two men also made history by encouraging Dr. Douglas Firth in the efforts that led to the founding of the Canadian Ski Patrol System by Firth in 1941.

One day in the winter of 1934-35, Larway happened to be in the office of a chocolate company when a salesman called in to report that he could not return to Toronto because he was snowbound. This alerted Larway to the good skiing possibilities, and he drove up on a Sunday with two carloads of fellow enthusiasts, including Sam Cliff and Fred Hall. Sam Cliff was President of the Toronto Ski Club from its inception until 1934, when he handed over the post to Hall. A leading Toronto businessman and a ski fanatic, Cliff was a friend of the renowned British ski authority Sir Arnold Lunn and was an honorary member of the Ski Club of Great Britain, whose activities took place mainly in Switzerland. On the trip led by Ross Larway there was no snow visible anywhere until the party arrived at Stayner, from where they could see the whitened hay fields on Blue Mountain that spelled out the LOL initials that were to become such a familiar landmark for approaching skiers. Upon arriving at Blue Mountain, Larway and his friends climbed up the O-Hill and skied it all day.

Inspired by their visit, the Torontonians kept a close watch on the operation that was being started up by local skiers and gradually increased their involvement. Cliff, Larway and Gib Temple attended the founding meeting of the Blue Mountain Ski Club and, as the club records indicate, "illustrated the art of skiing with motion pictures." The liaison culminated in the formation of the Blue Mountain Ski Club (1940) Inc., in which the TSC became a 50-percent partner and financed further expansion. The new organization assumed ownership of the original 150-acre

The south end of the resort before development, c. 1952. If we imagine some snow on the LOL hills, this is how they would have looked to Ross Larway and the two carloads of Toronto skiers when they were approaching Blue Mountain in 1935. Today they are the Big Baby, O-Hill and L-Hill.
– Courtesy: Jack MacMurchy, Credit: Herb Hall

Hermann Smith "Jackrabbit" Johannsen. The legendary ski coach and trail-cutter was born in Norway and came to Montreal in 1928. He lived to be over 111 years old. In 1940, at the request of the Toronto Ski Club, he surveyed the terrain at Blue Mountain and prepared a report on the layout of trails and tows.
– Courtesy: Canadian Ski Museum

Skiers aboard the Red Devil, c. 1942. The lack of snow prevented the inaugural opening of the Red Devil on January 9, 1937. However, the February 4, 1937, edition of the Enterprise-Bulletin *reported: "Sightseers and thrill-seekers may ride into the clouds in solid comfort. The Lift Committee has announced that tickets will sell at three for a quarter, with no additional amusement levy."*
– Courtesy: Collingwood Museum

Left: *Blue Mountain Ski Club members around their clubhouse stove, c. 1948. Left to right, rear: unknown, unknown, Myrtle Stoutenberg, Pat Stapleton, Joe Sorenson. Left to right, front: unknown, Eileen Kennedy, Charles Crysler, Ruth Smith.*
– Courtesy: Eileen Crysler

Right: *The Red Devil line-up, 1944. Toronto Ski Club pioneer Fred Hall claimed that he and three companions did 56 runs using the Red Devil one Sunday in the 1940s. This would have been impossible under crowded conditions such as the situation portrayed here.*
– Courtesy: Sue Boehm, Credit: Les Tucker

property and immediately bought another 200 acres from Colonel Carmichael for $3,000. This was the farm containing the south L-Hill and the O-Hill, two miles to the south of the main ski centre. The Blue Mountain Ski Club – the name was changed to the Collingwood Ski Club in 1961 – continued to exist as a separate organization that drew its members mainly from Collingwood. Blue Mountain Ski Club (1940) Inc. was governed by a board of six directors, three from each club.

In 1940 the Toronto Ski Club engaged the services of Jackrabbit Johannsen, who had already made himself a legend as a ski coach and trail-cutter in Quebec. During the 1930s Johannsen had laid out many of the trails in the Laurentians, disappearing for weeks into the bush, where he camped out in the snow. The TSC paid Johannsen $100 and expenses to come to Collingwood to survey the terrain and prepare a development plan. He determined the location of the main rope tow and some of the trails around it. By 1941 the two clubs had established rudimentary facilities on Blue Mountain: the log clubhouse, two rope tows and a sleigh tow.

Among the improvisations that were introduced by the Blue Mountain Ski Club, which had access to some talented technicians in the shipyard and the grain storage company Collingwood Terminals, the most interesting and durable contraption was the sleigh tow called the Red Devil. The Red Devil was installed on the Schuss in 1937. There were two sleighs, one being pulled to the top and the other coming down empty. Each sleigh carried nine skiers up the hill. Skiers took their skis off before boarding and either held them in their hands or placed them in a rack at the side of the sleigh. The tow was built by local ski enthusiasts, led by Fritz Loosli and Norman Boadway. The seats were manufactured in Boadway's basement. Careful calculations were made to allow skiers to sit flat while the tow was on an incline.

The local club was proud of its invention, which was also praised by the Toronto skiers. Toronto Ski Club pioneer Fred Hall later wrote that, by using the Red Devil one uncrowded Sunday, a foursome including himself, a skier appropriately named Wearie Williams, and two others were able to make 56 runs on the Schuss before fatigue set in. The tow was seldom this efficient, however. It could be knocked out for many hours when the cable froze into the track or broke in two, and there are stories of runaway sleighs that destroyed the tow shack at the bottom. According to one account, "bail out" was not an uncommon phrase to hear being bellowed across the hill as nine panic-stricken skiers jumped to safety. Nevertheless, the tow was a workhorse that would carry thousands of skiers up the hill for almost two decades before the finances of the struggling resort became strong enough to support more modern uphill transportation.

Mountain peaks above Jozo's chalet in Slovakia. Photograph by Jozo Weider, c. 1934. These mountains are part of the Carpathian range, which extends into Poland and the Ukraine. Jozo was an accomplished photographer and, while in Czechoslovakia, published a photo collection entitled Five Years as an Innkeeper. *Years later, after he had immigrated to Canada, he wrote a novel, never published, about the peasants and villagers of this little-known area of Europe.* – Courtesy: Mrs. Helen Weider, Credit: Jozo Weider

From the Carpathians to Collingwood

During the late 1930s when Blue Mountain skiers were bushwhacking on roughly cut trails and logging roads, building the Red Devil and swapping stories around their potbellied stove in the log clubhouse, a young European was also founding a ski resort, but in a little-known part of the world.

Jozo Weider was born in Zhilina, in the eastern or Slovak part of Czechoslovakia, in 1909. He was daring and enterprising from a young age. His youthful adventures included a period of service in the Czechoslovak Army. The army took note of his skiing ability and gave him time off for training and for competing in national and international Nordic competitions, in which he had great success. He loved kayaking on wild rivers and motorcycling. He rode his motorcycle at high speed through the Slovak countryside and used it to complete a long trip across Europe. At one point he joined a dance troupe that toured Austria and Germany; he performed Cossack dances dressed in the costume of a Russian peasant. He was impatient with formal schooling and did not complete his studies for a commerce degree in Vienna, where his father had sent

One of the Slovak peasants who helped Jozo build his chalet. Photograph by Jozo Weider, 1934. – Courtesy: Mrs. Helen Weider, Credit: Jozo Weider

Serenading guests at the chalet. Jozo with accordion.
– Courtesy: Mrs. Helen Weider

Jozo in the hope of preparing him to be an earnest businessman. He was good at languages and learned English, not knowing at the time how important that would be for him one day.

In his early 20s, much to his mother's disapproval, the brash young ski enthusiast borrowed some money from a local bank and went off to build a chalet in the mountains near his home town. These mountains were part of the Carpathian range, the Eastern European continuation of the Alps. The chalet was Jozo's home for most of the 1930s. From this base he carried on business as an innkeeper, mountain guide and photographer. The chalet could be reached only by a five-kilometre trek up a steep path, and supplies had to be carried by men or mules. When the chimney was being built, each guest was required to put at least one brick in his rucksack before beginning his ascent. The chalet accommodated about 40 guests, who were guided by Jozo on skiing and climbing expeditions, and entertained at night with his accordion-playing.

One of the guests was a young woman from the lowlands of Bohemia. She fell in love with both the mountains and Jozo. Jozo and Helen were married in one of the villages in the foothills below the chalet, and they lived in these tranquil surroundings for three years, until the political storms that were brewing in Europe made even this remote location a dangerous one. One night in February 1939, Jozo descended the path below his chalet and made his way through falling snow to the train station in the foothills. Although it was pitch dark, he knew the way by heart. He was not aware that he was leaving the chalet for the last time.

Jozo and Helen at their chalet. Their life at the chalet was related nostalgically to the Weider children by their parents. The chalet was located at the bottom of a mountain called the Rozsoutec, *at a place where three valleys met. After Jozo's death, Helen Weider published* Mountain Ballad, *a narrative poem about her romance with her husband and the mountains.* – Courtesy: Mrs. Helen Weider

The chalet, c. 1937. Jozo's sister-in-law Jarmila Uhrova remained in Czechoslovakia during the war and lived in the chalet. She sheltered partisans, who used it as a base for resistance against the German occupying forces. As the resistance movement gathered strength in the later stages of the war, Soviet officers from the advancing Red Army were parachuted into the mountains to direct the partisans. The chalet was blown up by the Germans in a reprisal action. Jarmila was hailed as a resistance heroine following the German defeat in 1945. With the help of Jozo, who sent funds from Canada, she rebuilt the chalet and restored it as a tourist centre. After the Communist takeover in Czechoslovakia in 1948 it was expropriated and run as a government operation. – Courtesy: Mrs. Helen Weider

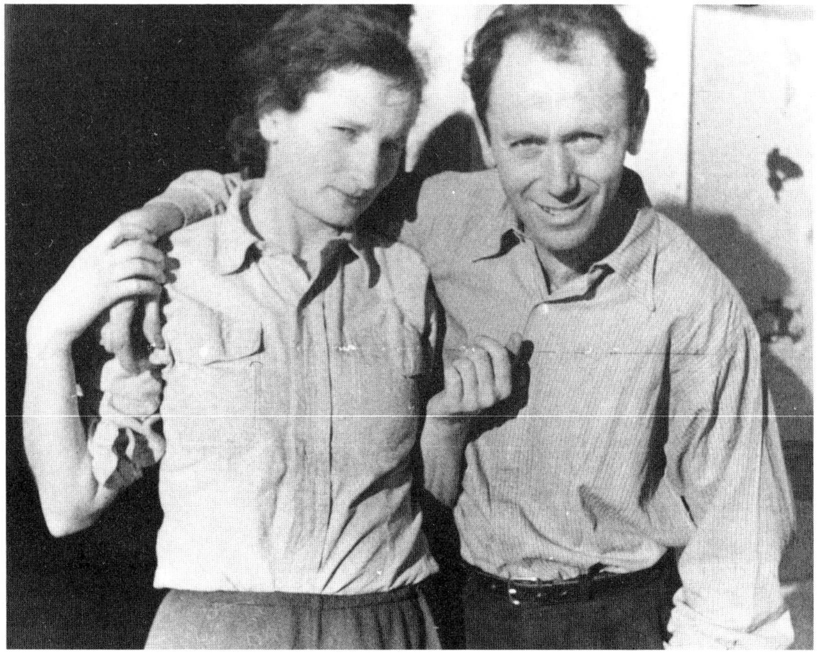

Jozo and Helen as colonists at Tupper Creek, British Columbia. After a 10-day train trip from Montreal, where their ship had landed, the immigrants arrived in the Peace River District, via Edmonton, on Jozo's 30th birthday, June 24, 1939. – Courtesy: Mrs. Helen Weider

The author with his father at Tupper Creek in the Peace River District, 1940. – Courtesy: Mrs. Helen Weider

He was heading for Britain to promote tourism for his resort and the region. In retrospect his project was an untimely one; the British university students whom he hoped to entice to his chalet ended up fighting the Germans instead. Jozo was still in Britain when the Nazis occupied Czechoslovakia in the spring of 1939. He decided not to return and declared himself a political refugee. He considered immigrating with his family to New Zealand but decided upon Canada when he heard about a colonization project organized by the Canadian government and the Canadian Pacific Railway.

The colonists' destination was Tupper Creek in the Peace River District of British Columbia, where they were allotted parcels of land for homesteading. Most of these immigrants were from the Sudetenland, the German-speaking part of northern Czechoslovakia, and, like Jozo, they were escaping from the Nazis. Jozo sent Helen an urgent telegram, asking her to join him as soon as possible. She packed up a few belongings and came to Britain, accompanied by their one-year-old son.

In the summer of 1939 the Weiders arrived in the Peace River District. Life was hard in this frontier settlement of 120 families. The Weiders lived in a one-room shanty. Drums of water had to be hauled on a wagon from a river several miles away. When winter came, Jozo left the settlement and travelled by train to the CPR's Chateau Frontenac, where he taught skiing through the 1939-40 season. He returned in the spring and found work on road gangs building the Alaska Highway.

After a year of living in these conditions Jozo concluded that he and his family faced a grim future in the backwoods, and he decided to go back into the ski business on a permanent basis. In the fall of 1940 he moved with his family to Quebec for another season of ski instruction. While instructing at the Alpine Inn at Ste. Marguerite, Jozo had a lunch-time conversation with a guest named Peter Campbell. Campbell, who was later appointed to the Senate, was a partner in a major Toronto law firm and director of several Canadian corporations. He was also counsel to Collingwood Terminals, which was headed by Norman Boadway, the ski pioneer who had built the first tows on Blue Mountain. Campbell was a risk-taker and good judge of men. He sized up Jozo as a hard worker and good promoter. He became Jozo's financial partner and backer throughout most of Jozo's career.

Jozo as Chief Instructor at the Alpine Inn, Ste. Marguerite, Quebec, season of 1940-41. He held permit no. 30 of the Canadian Ski School Ski Instructors' Alliance of the Canadian Amateur Ski Association. The comments by a superior in his licence book were, "Splendid teacher, good organizer."
– Courtesy: Mrs. Helen Weider

The author, at age three, in front of the Alpine Inn with his mother in the winter of 1941. His hat, parka and pants were handmade by his mother and much envied by other mothers of young skiers, as no ski clothing was manufactured for children at the time. Photograph by Jozo Weider.
– Courtesy: Mrs. Helen Weider, Credit: Jozo Weider

Campbell was following the events in Collingwood, where the Toronto Ski Club and the Blue Mountain Ski Club were developing ski facilities. With Campbell's support and the blessing of the two ski clubs, Jozo settled at Blue Mountain with his family at the end of the 1940-41 ski season. The two men formed Blue Mountain Resorts Limited, which in turn hired Jozo as instructor and sports director. They obtained nine acres of land from the clubs on which to build a lodge. Jozo was allocated a salary of $100 per month, "his necessary food and lodging," and a 25-percent share of the new company's profits.

Skiers, including Collingwood racer Marcella Plater (second from left), pose with CN No. 5033's engineer and fireman, 1948.
– Courtesy: Larry Plater

Skiers harmonize on the ski train to Collingwood, c. 1941.
– Courtesy: Sue Boehm, Credit: Les Tucker

Skiers arriving at the Craigleith station. This historic building has been preserved. It is now the Depot Restaurant, owned by Ken and Suyrea Knapman. – Courtesy: Township of Collingwood

PART II

The 1940s: Rough Beginnings

The Forties were a colourful period for the resort, highlighted by Jozo's first project, the Blue Mountain Lodge, and the ski trains, rope tows and the racing events organized by the Toronto Ski Club. They were also marked by the drive of Jozo Weider to take control of the resort's direction and to provide more aggressive management than that of the clubs. Blue Mountain became Jozo's permanent habitat, as he settled down to become a ski entrepreneur, colourful entertainer, promoter and a father of four children.

The First Lodge: Trains, Trails and Tows

Jozo vigorously launched his new enterprise the moment he arrived at Blue Mountain from Quebec in the spring of 1941. By the time the letters patent of Blue Mountain Resorts Limited were taken out in October 1941, he already had the roof on Blue Mountain Lodge, which he had immediately begun building with the assistance of local farmers, carpenters and tradesmen. The project was launched with the help of $4,000 that Jozo had borrowed from a wealthy American industrialist who had been a guest at Ste. Marguerite the previous season and who had befriended him. The Lodge could accommodate 38 people and became the main facility for overnight guests visiting the resort and the scene of much après-ski revelry. Rates in 1942 were $7 a day, including meals. Advertisements boasted of a major improvement in 1942: hot and cold running water in some of the rooms.

Jozo and his workers were frantically finishing the interior of the Lodge as the 1941-42 ski season opened. Bunk beds for the guests were being installed even as these guests were making their way to the Lodge from the train station. Alex McVicar, a long-time ski patroller at Blue Mountain, remembers being snowbound in the Lodge for three days when the road to Craigleith Station and Highway 26 was closed by a blizzard. He and other guests at the Lodge took turns skiing out to the highway to pick up food supplies. Much of the cooking was done by Myrtle Plater, wife of local farmer Don Plater. "Slice the roast beef so thinly that you can see Blue Mountain through it when you hold it up to the window," she was instructed by Jozo.

For almost five decades the Lodge was a landmark at the north end of the resort. Its low sloped roof lines, decorated shutters, and combination of white stucco and darkly stained half-log walls recreated the Alpine-village style of Switzerland and the Tyrol. The setting at the foot of the northernmost part of Blue Mountain was idyllic. Seclusion was provided by the very long laneway that led almost to the edge of the mountain. The Lodge was framed by towering elm and basswood trees, and the hardwood forest at the edge of the clearing provided a stunning backdrop when the leaves turned in the fall. A fast-flowing creek ran down the mountain beside the Lodge and on through farm fields to Georgian Bay.

The beauty of the Lodge and its setting was accentuated in paintings by Walter Trier, an artist-illustrator of world renown. Trier was born in Prague in 1890 and studied art in Munich and Berlin. He emerged as one of Europe's leading caricaturists and practitioners of humorous art. He loved animals and published many children's books of animal sketches and stories. Trier and his wife, Helen, immigrated to Toronto from Britain in 1947 and settled at Blue Mountain two years later in a house and studio built for them by Jozo.

In the 1940s many of the guests of both the Lodge and the resort arrived by train. The fun and camaraderie on the train made the three-hour train trip a desirable alternative to car travel on rough, early highways. Collingwood and Craigleith were accessible by regularly scheduled CNR passenger trains, and in addition, special excursions were organized by the Toronto Ski Club. In 1940 the TSC ran a gala excursion to celebrate the New Year and christen the new rope tow designed by Norman Boadway. The train left Union Station at 7:45 on New Year's Eve and arrived in Collingwood three hours later for a dance and New Year's Eve party at the Maple Leaf Hall. The revellers were transported to the dance hall by the Collingwood Fire Department, accompanied by a brass band. After the party, a few hours of sleep could be obtained in the sleeping cars, which were parked at a siding next to the main street. In the early morning the cars were gently pulled to Craigleith, where the skiers disembarked for a day on the slopes. The entire excursion, including the round-trip train ticket and breakfast, lunch and dinner on New Year's Day, cost $4.35. The excursion was repeated the following year. This time there was a New Year's Day breakfast in the Blue Mountain Lodge, which had just been completed by Jozo. There was continuous partying on the train.

Those unable to afford a sleigh ride from the Craigleith Depot to the hills trudge up Sand Hill on Blue Mountain Road. – Courtesy: Sue Boehm, Credit: Les Tucker

Skiers arriving by train are met by horse-drawn sleighs.
– Courtesy: Township of Collingwood

Sleigh ride to the LOL hills, 10 cents. Left to right: Wearie Williams, Les Tucker, Ottilie Galbraith and Fred Hall, c. 1941.
– Courtesy: Sue Boehm, Credit: Les Tucker

Morrill's Ski Shop located at Blue Mountain's north end, c. 1948.
– Courtesy: Collingwood Museum

Back to the slopes after refreshments, c. 1943. Left to right: Art Yates, Pat Yates, Emelia [?], Millie Metcalfe and Bill Spencer.
– Courtesy: Art & Pat Yates, Credit: R.W. Harrington

During one of the trips a collapsible organ was carried on board and the baggage car became a music centre. The ensuing songfest spread to the coaches in the middle of the train.

January 5, 1941, marked the inauguration of the Blue Mountain Ski Special, which left Union Station at 7:25 every Sunday morning during the ski season. Returning skiers could board the train at Craigleith at 4:45 p.m. and be back in Toronto by early evening. Those who wanted a longer day could return by regular coach, which left Craigleith at 7:20 p.m. Almost 200 skiers were on board for the inaugural expedition. Train fare, including the return to Toronto, was $1.95.

The special ski trains were discontinued after 1942 because of the priority attached to moving war supplies, but skiers could still use the regular passenger service, which ran until 1960. During the war years, skiers had to sacrifice valuable gas ration coupons to get to the resort. Special trains ran again in the 1947 season. Trains arriving at the Craigleith station in the 1940s were met by horse-drawn sleighs, or by a war-surplus army truck driven by Jozo or one of his employees. Sleighs were also sent from the Bayview Ski Trails, an operation run by the Doherty brothers on a slope north of the Blue Mountain resort. Like several other commercial operations attempted on the escarpment, Bayview did not survive. Its hill was eventually taken over by the private Craigleith Ski Club.

These early skiers were a hardy bunch, and many refused to pay the 25 cents for the ride on the sleigh. Instead, they shouldered their gear and trekked up "sand hill" and on to Blue Mountain, one mile to the south. When they got to the mountain, whether from the train or by car, most skiers would head for the Blue Mountain Lodge or the log clubhouse, which had been in use since 1936 and which continued to serve as a base facility throughout the Forties. The clubhouse was close to the bottom of the two tows, the sleigh tow and the Grand Central rope tow. There were no washrooms at the base of the area and skiers had to make do with only one or two outdoor privies. According to Ross Grinnell, who skied the area in these years, a woman was sitting in an outhouse at the bottom of the Schuss when a runaway ski took off from high on the hill. It struck the flimsy little building with such force that it pierced the wall and came within inches of impaling the terrified occupant.

Immediately to the south of the clubhouse was a ski shop and repair service operated by Alf Morrill and his son, Lawrence. The Morrills owned a carpentry business in Collingwood and operated the ski shop as a sideline. They crafted their own skis and sold them at the resort. "They had steel edges and were among the best equipment you could buy anywhere at the time," remembers Bert Brydon, who bought a pair in the 1930s and used them until a terrific crack-up caused him to put them away forever.

The rugged skied to the O-Hill, but these skiers preferred to preserve their energies for the downhill run, c. 1951. – Courtesy: Art & Pat Yates, Credit: Les Tucker

The centre of activity, c. 1948. On the right is the log cabin, renovated by the Blue Mountain Ski Club for a clubhouse in 1936. At some point in the 1940s a frame addition was added on the north side to provide more food service. On the left is the Morrill ski shop. Both buildings were later removed, but most of the clubhouse was resurrected as part of a chalet on Georgian Bay between Craigleith and Thornbury. – Courtesy: Collingwood Museum

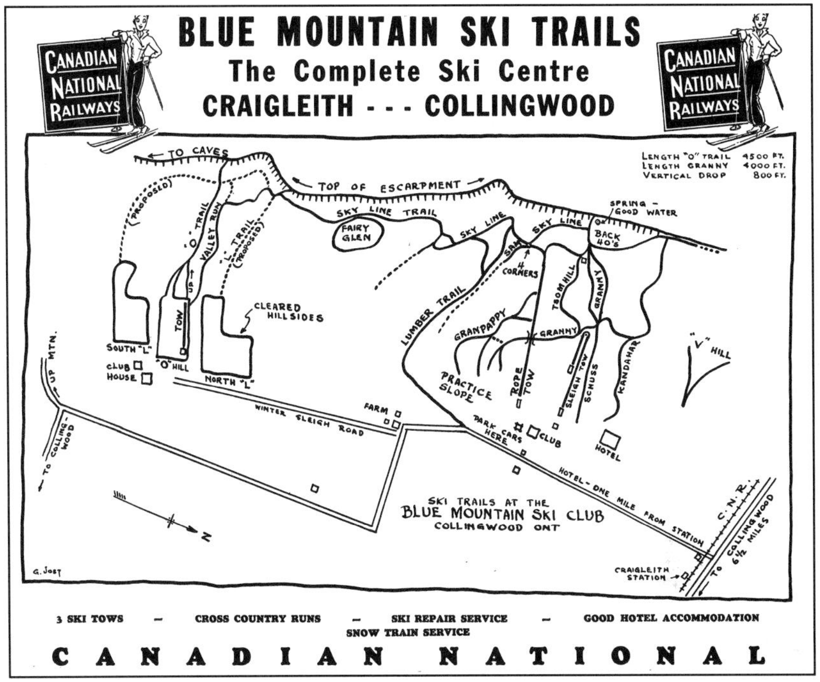

George Jost's c. 1942 Blue Mountain Trail Map.
– Courtesy: Paul Hughes, Credit: George Jost

A sign in front of the clubhouse advertised the sleigh for the O-Hill, two miles away. Farmers – usually John Currie and Art Horner – would park their sleighs and wait for a full load before heading for the O-Hill or the train station. In 1948 the ride to the O-Hill cost 10 cents one way.

Considering the primitive condition of the resort in the 1940s, the skiers had a reasonably good variety of runs from which to make their selection. The choices were outlined on a map prepared by George Jost for the CNR, which was advertising the resort in connection with the ski trains. Jost was a racing coach with the Toronto Ski Club in the early 1940s. In 1933 he had won a prestigious British downhill in Switzerland, the Roberts Kandahar, and he was considered an expert on everything about Blue Mountain when he was on the scene. A fitness fanatic, he recommended that those skiers who arrived by train should refrain from riding to the hill on a sleigh and instead make the one-mile trip on foot in order to get warmed up before making downhill runs.

Jost's map, which is now a collectors' item, was useful in outlining the trails and layout of the resort in the early 1940s. The main runs were the Schuss and the Granny, which could be reached from the sleigh tow or the rope tow. The rope tow was rebuilt several times until finally replaced by a pomalift in 1955. The original rope tow was over 2,000 feet long and passed through an embankment and under a narrow bridge. When descending the upper Granny it was difficult not to pick up considerable speed before approaching the bridge where the rope tow was crossed in order to get to the easier slopes below. So fearful was this point in the run that it was dubbed the "Oh Jesus bridge." Around 1946 the bridge was removed by dynamite, and the area around it was smoothed over, allowing an easier run to the lower Granny and even gentler Practice Slope. "Even your 'Granny' should be able to run it now," boasted Toronto Ski Club President Len Meyer in his pre-season message in 1946. At the same time, the Schuss was widened and made ideal for slalom racing.

Above the Granny, and converging with the Granny near the bridge, was the Tsomhll Trail, a narrow downhill racing trail with a fade-away corner where many racers came to grief. The name – a typographical

Skiers line up at the Grand Central rope tow. The original rope tow was built in 1940 but was redesigned several times. – Courtesy: Collingwood Museum

Skiers quench their thirst in a Blue Mountain stream, c. 1949.
– Courtesy: Doug & Katie Wallace

The rope tow on O-Hill, seen here in 1951, was originally opened in January 1941. – Courtesy: Bev Beecham Gordon

Photographed by Sportsworld *in 1940, John Dinnick of the Toronto Ski Club demonstrates three techniques that were handy for explorations away from prepared slopes. Left to right: Gelandesprung, Jump Turn and Christianna. The Gelandesprung was recommended for clearing fences and brush. "It was also the favourite method," cautioned the journal, "of breaking ski tips and skiers' necks." An all-around athlete, Dinnick was intercollegiate heavyweight boxing champion at the University of Toronto and also played golf and tennis. He took up skiing seriously at the age of 12, when he was left a pair of skis in a relative's will. After service overseas with the Royal Canadian Artillery he became a long-time skier at Blue Mountain, occupying a chalet at the north of the resort.*
– Courtesy: Ross Wilson

nightmare for sports reporters and brochure writers, and converted to Tsom Hill on the CNR map – was made up of the first letters of the surnames of the early Blue Mountain Ski Club executive: Trill (Bud), Smart (John), Orr (Jim), McCaul (Mary), Harvie (Doug), Loosli (Fritz), and Leinster (Gilford). This trail was phased out later in the Forties.

A winter sleigh road led south to the LOL hills. Only the O-Hill was regularly used, as it was serviced by a rope tow. The fields and forests between the north L-Hill and the Lumber Trail remained undeveloped until the 1950s, when Jozo Weider purchased the Kinsey and Plater farms. They were seldom skied on in the 1940s, but a rent of $25 per season was paid for each of the two farms.

While most of the skiers stuck to trails serviced by tows, there were some who enjoyed the adventure of touring or bushwhacking into the untracked territory. Advanced skiers were trained in making effortless jump turns over logs or fences, christying strongly through breakable crust and stemming to check their speed on a steep and narrow path or logging road. From the top of the Back 40s they could ski down the partially cleared Lumber Trail and explore the wooded slopes to the south instead of returning to the tows at the north. On one such jaunt Ross Larway had trouble steering his skis while burdened with a heavy rucksack and ended up in a manure-strewn barnyard, where he smacked into the belly of a cow. The "Sky Line Trail" was little more than a narrow footpath, but it was sometimes used as an upper route to the O-Hill. Touring was facilitated by cable bindings which allowed removal of the cables from downpull lugs under the heel of the boot. When the cables were disengaged from the lugs, the touring skier could lift up his heels and stride forward easily. Rucksacks were usually carried, and on a sunny spring day a touring party might stop beside one of the sparkling mountain streams to lunch and bask in the sunshine.

Rope tows were the most reliable and widely used method of transporting skiers up the hill in the early years. The first rope tow at Blue Mountain was designed by Norman Boadway and built in 1940 immediately to the east of the sleigh tow and in front of the log clubhouse of the Blue Mountain Ski Club. Demonstrating Boadway's engineering skills, the device was powered by a two-ton truck mounted on steel rails so that the slack of the rope could be easily adjusted. Despite this fine tuning, shorter skiers were at a disadvantage; the rope was too high for them and lifted them off the ground near the end of the line. The long length of the tow prompted George Jost to warn skiers not to be discouraged at the beginning of the season when their forearm muscles were weak. By the end of the season they would end up with their right arms much stronger than their left arms. Jost lauded the efficiency of the rope tow, pointing out that a keen skier could get in 12 runs per hour, or a total of 72 runs in six hours of skiing. At 500 vertical feet per run, he

Skiers sun on the "V" Hill, 1949. Left to right: Marg Gooch, Katie Forsyth, Bert Byer, Lee Jones, Chuck Gooch, Frank Whitehead and Freddie Gooch.
– Courtesy: Doug & Katie Wallace

Jozo on rope, c. 1948.
– Courtesy: Blue Mountain Resorts Limited

Left to right: Tom McGoey, Ross Wilson, Art Yates and Doc Pearson in front of a rope tow, c. 1948. Barely visible are the axles of the World War II Bren gun carrier that was used to power the tow. The body of the machine was inside the tow shack.
– Courtesy: Art & Pat Yates

"Swedish veteran Retep Llimsgnik" (Peter Kingsmill) practises on the Schuss, c. 1949. – Courtesy: David Cochran

could get in 36,000 vertical feet per day and thereby obtain six times as much skiing as in climbing the Alps or Rockies. "Why go to the Rocky Mountains to ski?" asked Jost. "Come on up to the Blue Mountain in Collingwood."

Although Jost was forgetting that there also were tows in the Rockies, his observation had some truth in it. The rope tows were speedier than the Red Devil and allowed a skier to log a great amount of vertical feet if he had the stamina. Perhaps inspired by Jost's enthusiasm, Jozo built several additional rope tows during his 30 years at Blue Mountain.

Tracked armoured vehicles called Bren gun carriers were purchased from war-surplus merchants for around $700 each and run up the hills, where they were stripped of their tracks and used to power the tows.

Some skiers complained that trying to grab a rope when it was wet was like trying to catch a greased pig. In order to make the ride easier, a few skiers used a metal gripping device to clamp onto the rope. This caused problems, as the clamp could freeze shut during the ride or it could cut or damage the rope, and the grippers were prohibited. In a later decade, a Blue Mountain rope tow operator fell asleep in the tow shack and did not notice when a woman fell in the track and was burned by the rope. When she irately knocked on the door and complained, he came out and pointed to a sign on the building saying "No Tow Grippers Allowed." "You see that sign, lady?" he countered. "It says, 'No tow *gripers* allowed.' "

The "hemp horrors," as some called the rope tows, were gradually phased out and replaced by pomalifts, T-bars and chairlifts. However, a beginner rope tow was operated at the southeast corner of the Apple Bowl as late as 1986, at an inflation-beating price of $1 per day. This beginner area is now served by the Easy Street Chairlift.

Downhill and slalom racing were an important pastime for skiers during the 1940s, especially in connection with club activity. Because of the relatively underdeveloped nature of recreational skiing, expert skiers were more apt to seek their thrills by spending part of their weekends racing in club championships and provincial or intercollegiate meets. Peter Kingsmill was a popular figure around the Blue Mountain Lodge in the later 1940s. Kingsmill has maintained a long association with the sport, beginning with his days as a racer with the University of Toronto. He was a whirlwind of activity on the ski scene, holding down, among other positions, the chairmanship of the Toronto Ski Club Racing Section. In addition to organizing races, he also competed, winning the Toronto Ski Club Championship in 1949 on the strength of two flawless slalom runs on the Schuss. He was at the forefront of many high jinks around Blue Mountain, distinguished by his high-pitched yodel and his Swiss mountaineering hat with a feather in it.

Kingsmill also wrote a column called "Skimming the Slopes" for the *Globe and Mail.* When describing his own victories, he referred to "Swedish veteran Retep Llimsgnik," spelling his own name backwards. This prank aroused the wrath of the sports editor, Jim Vipond, when Vipond eventually caught on.

Another fine skier of the period was Doug Mann of the Toronto Ski Club. He frequented the hills around Blue Mountain after returning from war service overseas. He married a leading woman competitor, Peg Pugsley, also from the Toronto Ski Club. Mann was known for his excellent technique and his racing ability. A superb Alpine competitor, he was only 16 when he won the Dominion Slalom Championship in 1936.

Contestants gather at the Blue Mountain Lodge for the first Yellingtimber (Collingwood) Mudslides Gluevine Race. Master of ceremonies was Peter Kingsmill (far left).
– Courtesy: Peter Kingsmill

Ontario's leading woman racer in the early 1940s, Elizabeth Snively, 1942.
– Courtesy: Sue Boehm, Credit: Les Tucker

Hill grooming in the 1940s.
Jozo tramps the hill in preparation
for the 1942 Ontario Ladies Championships.
– Courtesy: Sue Boehm, Credit: Les Tucker

Doug Mann of the Toronto Ski Club in action at Blue Mountain, 1947. Mann shows the proper knee and shoulder movement in the classical rotation method. – Courtesy: Sue Boehm, Credit: Les Tucker

Ottilie Galbraith, author of the "Fashion Thru The Snowflakes" column, c. 1940. – Courtesy: Sue Boehm, Credit: Les Tucker

Later, as a member of the McGill Redbirds, he earned numerous national and international honours, including two wins in the Quebec Kandahar and an astonishing victory over the nearly invincible American ace Dick Durrance. He was slated to represent Canada in the Olympic games, but when war broke out he went overseas and served as a flight lieutenant in the RCAF.

In 1947 Doug Mann was photographed at Blue Mountain demonstrating technique for the benefit of a group of juniors from the Toronto Ski Club. Three years later he was fatally injured in an automobile accident. The Doug Mann trophy was established by the club in his memory. "Doug Mann was one of Canada's all-time skiing greats," wrote Peter Kingsmill on the occasion of Mann's tragic death in 1950.

Women skiers such as Gertrude Hall, Betty McGoey and Ottilie Galbraith played a prominent role in the development of the sport in the 1940s. During the war years many of them were without their men. They organized catering for special events, wrote newsletters and assisted in the running of races. Several became fine competitors in their own right. Elizabeth Snively was introduced to the sport at the age of four in the late 1920s, on the original trails used by the Toronto Ski Club at Summit. She was taught by her father, Major Alex Snively, an enthusiastic sportsman and telemark expert who had helped found the Toronto Ski Club in 1924. A diehard traditionalist, the Major wrote to *The Ski-Runner* in 1941 objecting to the increasing use of downhill bindings and the removal of telemarking from the tests required for certificates in skiing proficiency. His daughter did not share his concerns and became a dedicated downhiller. After Summit, Elizabeth mastered the more challenging hills of Blue Mountain and emerged as Ontario's leading woman racer in the early 1940s. In 1941 she defeated the powerful McGill Ski Club women's team in a slalom race at the Seigniory Club in Quebec. At a Quebec-Ontario meet at Blue Mountain in 1943, she won the slalom over the famous Quebec racer Gaby Pleau and placed second in the downhill on the difficult and seldom-used Tsomhll Trail, again defeating Pleau, who placed third.

After her racing career Elizabeth Snively Dunbar continued recreational skiing at Blue Mountain. She was part of an informal group of enthusiasts who called themselves "Jozo's Bozos." They stayed at Blue Mountain Lodge, the Martin farmhouse near the north end of the resort, and later in the Carmichael farmhouse at the foot of the O-Hill. Mrs. Dunbar has skied at Blue Mountain throughout the entire 50-year period covered in this book.

Fellow racers, Connie Sparrow and Helen Weider, 1949.
– Courtesy: Connie Sparrow Trusler

Another formidable competitor was Jozo's daughter Helen Weider. Helen's ski career blossomed in the 1950s, but she got her start with the women of the Forties, frequently defeating racers who were two or three times her age. Born when the Weiders were homesteading in the Peace River District, she was only eight years old when photographed at a meet with Connie Sparrow in 1949. At age 11, three years later, she won the Toronto Ski Club Ladies Championship.

Connie Sparrow competed in numerous intercollegiate meets in Ontario and Quebec as a member of the University of Toronto women's ski team. She and her brother Bob were habitual guests at the Blue Mountain Lodge or the Weider farmhouse and did various tasks to help pay for their accommodation. On one occasion, Bob Sparrow, who was wearing "long-thong" bindings (long leather straps wrapped around the boots), refused to remove his skis as was customary when boarding the sleigh tow. He instead stretched himself into the ski rack on the side of the sleigh. Mayhem occurred when Jozo, who was operating the tow, mistakenly put it into reverse. There was a mighty jerking, and Connie and the other riders were soon tangled up with Bob and his equipment. The occupants ended up underneath the sleigh and narrowly escaped being injured. No one was allowed to wear skis on the sleigh after that incident.

Pat Curtis sporting an Irving ski suit, c. 1946.
– Courtesy: Sue Boehm, Credit: Les Tucker

Along with many other skiers from this era of the Lodge and sleigh tow, Connie Sparrow (later Mrs. George Trusler) joined the Osler Bluff Ski Club, which was formed in 1949.

Looking good on the slopes was important to the women of the Forties, who were intent on combining practicality with fashion. For only $4 or $5 they could purchase a pair of good-quality ski boots in white leather to assert their femininity, but reinforced by steel shafts and extra-thick soles to provide support while charging through a slalom course. A pair of lined gabardine slacks with permanent creases and zippered pockets could be obtained for less than $6, and a smart waterproof jacket of gabardine or grenfell cloth cost about the same. Haversacks made of light waterproof cloth in plain or plaid were handy for packing both ski waxes and cosmetics.

A leading authority on ski fashions was Ottilie Galbraith, who wrote a column on the subject in *The Ski-Runner*. Among her recommendations was a detachable parka made of waterproof grenfell cloth and lined with white fur "to make you glamorous even in the rawest weather." To keep one's hands warm there were mitts with white bunny fur on the back and a hard leather palm which could take punishment on rope tows. She was also taken with a reversible coat that she had seen at Eaton's. It was lipstick-red corduroy on the one side and a plaid of Gordon tartan on the other. A practical item in a straight tailored cut with large patch pockets, it was ideal for riding from the clubhouse on the sleigh or just travelling to the resort by car.

Fashion plates, 1942. Left to right: Mary Graham, Pat Langley and Freda Laidlaw. – Courtesy: Sue Boehm, Credit: Les Tucker

Jozo Weider shortly after his arrival at Blue Mountain, 1941.
– Courtesy: Sue Boehm, Credit: Les Tucker

While the skiers of the Forties enjoyed the trains, the Red Devil and the sleighs to Blue Mountain Lodge, it was a busy and difficult time for Jozo. At first his main preoccupation was Blue Mountain Lodge, but by the middle of the decade he was in the process of integrating all phases of the operation under his management. He personally met the ski train when it arrived at Craigleith station, then transported his guests back to the Lodge, where he entertained them with his accordion. He also supervised the cutting and widening of trails and the installation of new rope tows. For now, he had to keep much of the old equipment running while dreaming up new schemes to finance his ambitious development plans.

Manager, Promoter and Farmer

Toward the end of the 1940s Jozo was well on his way to becoming an institution around Blue Mountain and the area. This charismatic man had a great impact on people and events in his time. Jozo loved skiing, which he did with great zest, yodelling loudly from the top of the mountain and leaping off moguls or making turns on one ski in a carefree style. His broad face was distinguished by high cheekbones and rather fierce-looking green eyes. He was very observant and quickly took in every detail while driving wildly along the dirt road at the foot of the mountain,

A promotional photo by the CNR, *1948. Jozo tends the horse as Don and Myrtle Plater pose as grandparents meeting their daughter Marcella Plater.*
– Courtesy: Larry Plater, Credit: Canadian National Railways

Jozo's promotional skills were put to work as soon as he arrived in Canada. Here he is shown taking to the air in Slovak national costume while teaching at the Chateau Frontenac in the winter of 1939-40. The photo caught the fancy of an American reporter and made the New York Times.
– Courtesy: Mrs. Helen Weider

with a huge cloud of dust pluming after him. He would personally inspect all parts of his ski and tourist operation, and he made it his policy to be in close touch with both his customers and employees. He refused to be a desk-bound executive and had little patience for paperwork. Although many of his plans were very elaborate, they were usually worked out in his head; he thought and worked with great speed. Later, in the 1950s, his secretary Dorcas Watsham became indispensable to him, handling many of the administrative and legal details and much of Jozo's personal business as well. The two shared an office, and their frequent arguments would sometimes lead to shouting matches. Fortunately for the harmony of the staff, Jozo was usually on the move and seldom at his desk.

Jozo was a flamboyant promoter, knowing that he could get free publicity by stunts such as dressing up in Slovak national costume and holding an accordion in his hands while skiing. He was a witty and irreverent after-dinner speaker, seldom taking the time to prepare, and getting by with spontaneous jokes and anecdotes. Although his English was shaky when he first arrived, it improved quickly, as he obtained plenty of practice; he never turned down a chance to address a gathering. His Czech accent, which was heavy in the early years and never totally disappeared, was an asset rather than a handicap; it fortified the exotic image of the man. The local inhabitants, in particular, were amused by this wild-speaking foreigner with the crazy idea of making their farming community a tourist mecca for all of Ontario. "The Weiders were the first foreign people most of us had ever met," muses Ken Skelton, who became Jozo's machinist and outdoor manager, and who worked with him for a lifetime. "It was as if someone had landed here from the moon."

On one occasion Jozo gave a dressing down to a group of farmers at a gathering in Thornbury, accusing them of maintaining a double standard, poisoning the air by spraying their apple trees while at the same time voting against his application for a liquor licence for the resort. They applauded him, but the licence continued to be denied. On matters involving the Toronto Ski Club, Jozo was especially combative and would go over the heads of the club directors by grabbing the microphone and appealing directly to packed audiences at the club's annual meeting at the Eaton Centre. There was one predominant message which he hammered home again and again. He was driven by a desire to get Ontarians to love winter and the thrills of his favourite winter sport. In countless speeches, letters and brochures he encouraged Ontarians to take up skiing instead of going south to Florida to escape the cold and snow.

Jozo, his wife and his four children – twin daughters had been born a year and a half after the family's arrival from Quebec – lived most of their years at Blue Mountain in a farmhouse near the foot of the slopes. When Jozo arrived to take command of the resort, the local community was a sleepy little farming enclave. Craigleith had once been a busy place. The

The future Weider farm, viewed from the Granny, c. 1937-38. The farm on the left, owned by David Bouie, was bought by Jozo in 1946. It was the centre of an active farming operation that included the hills of the resort. On the right is the 100-acre Martin farm, owned by the Goodchild family and later purchased by the Martineks of Tyrolean Village.
– Courtesy: Collingwood Museum

industrious Scottish engineer Sandford Fleming (later knighted as a result of his efforts to organize a national railway and his invention of standardized time zones) had settled part of his family there in the 1850s. The Flemings had made Craigleith a hive of activity in connection with railway construction around Collingwood, carrying on farming, sawmilling and quarrying. There had been an inn, tavern and post office as well as the railway station. By the 1940s, however, it was hardly a village any more. There remained a small cluster of families, primarily engaged in farming and descended from the original settlers: the Flemings, Dohertys, Goodchilds, Campbells, Kinseys and Platers.

Members of these families served on the school board, organized communal threshing bees and carried on a "snow club," an informal organization in which each farmer undertook to attempt to clear the public road in front of his farm. The heavy snowdrifts on the road from Highway 26 to Blue Mountain were always a problem and hampered Jozo's ski operation until he persuaded the township council to provide a plowing service. In earlier years the road had been impassable in winter. John Goodchild remembers that because of the bad road conditions in Craigleith in the 1930s, his parents boarded him in Collingwood for entire winters throughout his high-school years. When ski operations started to become more important, many of the local farmers were glad to supplement their incomes by taking weekend jobs at the resort or the private ski clubs, and by the 1950s several were taking advantage of rising land prices to sell all or part of their lands for ski operations or subdivisions.

Although hardly any of the Craigleith landowners were able to make a living as full-time farmers, during the 1940s and 1950s farming was an important sideline for many families, including the Weiders. Their farm was located near the entrance to Blue Mountain Lodge and could be viewed from the north slopes of the resort. Between their farm and the mountain was the Martin farm, which was owned by Joseph Goodchild before being purchased by Joe and Bill Martinek, the Czechoslovakian immigrants who founded the Tyrolean Village resort on nearby lands. In the 1940s many skiers stayed in the stone farmhouse now occupied by Joe and Brenda Martinek. When the Weiders arrived in 1941, they lived in a cabin beside Blue Mountain Lodge. They also rented the stone Martin house for a few seasons in order to make room for guests at the Lodge, and finally moved to the 100-acre farm that Jozo purchased from David Bouie in 1946 for $4,000.

The farm became the Weiders' home for the next 21 years and was also used as a work centre for the resort. Rooms in the farmhouse were rented to guests when the Lodge was overflowing. Part of the barn was used as a machine shop for the assembly and partial fabrication of lifts, including the first modern lift, the North Poma, in 1955.

The farm provided the base for a very self-sufficient resort operation. After picking apples from the orchards on Blue Mountain, Jozo would load barrels of them on a resort truck, which he would drive to Sudbury or other places in the North. With the proceeds from the apples he would purchase a load of scrawny cattle and take them home to the barn, where they would be fattened over the winter. Hay was harvested from the hills and stored in the barn.

In front of the barn was a chicken house that was stuffed with sawdust to store blocks of ice. The sawdust was produced in a sawmill that Jozo built beside the farmhouse. The sawmill was used to cut up logs cleared from the hills. The crude boards that were produced were used as cladding for the shacks that housed the rope tows. The ice was delivered by Jozo to cottagers on Georgian Bay who used the blocks in ice-boxes. Some of the animals on the Weider farm served as models for the artist Walter Trier. His favourite was the floppy-eared springer spaniel, Topsy, who followed the Weider children all over Craigleith. She had many puppies and greatly increased the canine population.

Jozo Weider and Ken Skelton were very creative in improvising mechanical devices for both farming and resort operations. Among their inventions were a railway for launching boats into Georgian Bay and a

The Craigleith School class of 1944-45. Left to right: John Kinsey, George Weider, Margaret Campbell, George Fleming, Don Plater and Helen Weider. Rear: Mrs. Sadie McLean (teacher). – Courtesy: Don Plater

water ski tow which was tried out unsuccessfully on the resort's water reservoir "Lake Jozo." They were also resourceful at scavenging among old engines and discarded vehicles for parts. Jozo was always on the lookout for bargain equipment. He haunted war-surplus stores, bankruptcy sales and the yards of the salvage merchants. The Weiders' yard was always littered with used restaurant equipment, pieces of steel and vehicle parts that he had purchased. In the 1970s Jozo's daughter Anna and her husband cleaned up the grounds and renovated the century farmhouse for their own use.

During their years at Craigleith the four Weider children got their primary education at the one-room school near the Craigleith train station. In the collection of Donald Plater is a 1945 photo of him and his classmates, including my sister Helen and me. Helen was only four years old and was sent to the school a year early to rescue it from being closed. As a result of the dwindling population of the farming community, the class of 1945 had only six pupils in it. When softball teams came to visit from neighbouring schools, players had to be borrowed from the visitors to make up the home team. Proudly holding a blackboard with the school's name on it was George Fleming. A descendant of the original Flemings through a brother of Sir Sandford, he lived in a handsome brick house next to the school. The school had been built in 1862 on a lot donated by Andrew G. Fleming, Sir Sandford's father. White limestone for the walls was obtained from the Flemings' quarry nearby. George went on to adopt the profession of his gifted ancestor, Sir Sandford Fleming, graduating from the University of Toronto as a civil engineer, but he remained involved with Craigleith long after his school days were over. About 100 years after his great-grandfather Andrew G. Fleming had proposed a subdivision for Craigleith, George designed and implemented a major development project, Georgian Woodlands, to the northwest of the Depot Restaurant and former railway station.

Donald Plater has remained in the area, farming his land near Alpine Ski Club and joining Blue Mountain's staff on a part-time basis.

Jozo always said that it was for his family that he worked so hard, and he was a generous husband and father, although quick-tempered and ready to scold. On his first trip to the Colorado Rockies, he was so enthralled with seeing real mountains again – they reminded him of his old haunts in Slovakia – that he turned his car around and drove the 2,000 miles back to Blue Mountain to pick up his family so that they could return with him and share the pleasure. While he was very concerned that the children take their education seriously, he was not averse to plucking them out of school for a day if there was a sudden snowfall that dumped 10 inches of powder on the mountain.

Throughout the 1940s Blue Mountain Resorts was in precarious financial condition and frequently behind in loan payments to the Toronto Ski Club. From the moment Jozo launched his first project he was short of working capital and was chronically late in paying his bills. In November 1941 he applied to the Toronto Ski Club for a loan of $500 to complete work for the coming season. The loan was authorized with the stipulation that it was to be the last. Two weeks later he applied again, this time for $1,500 to complete the Lodge. The club loaned him only $200 and in return received eight shares in Blue Mountain Resorts, valued at $25 each. More shares were acquired by the club over the years until 1986, when in its final year as a shareholder the TSC owned 12,450 common shares representing an eight-percent holding in the company.

Other parties became shareholders by such conversions of debt to equity. Frequently it was an ordeal for Jozo to meet a payroll or a bill from a contractor or local merchant, and a share issue was the only way of satisfying the obligation. Jozo was rescued by his talents in inspiring confidence among his lenders and getting them to invest; they could have foreclosed or sued. The company's minutes show that in 1947 the Bryan Lumber Company of Collingwood received 40 preference shares in lieu of $4,000 that was owed to it. Other local merchants also obtained shares in this way. Guests at the lodge were encouraged to purchase some shares. Among the prospects was a wealthy woman who loved Limburger cheese. When Jozo heard that she was coming for a weekend he urgently asked the staff whether they had Limburger cheese on hand. Myrtle Plater, who was managing the kitchen, dared not admit that they hadn't liked the smell of the cheese and had thrown it out the window. She directed a frantic hunt for the cheese, which was dug out of a snowbank, thawed out, and served that evening.

In 1941 the company began its long relationship with the Canadian Imperial Bank of Commerce. Many years later, a senior CIBC executive and future chairman, Donald Fullerton, broke his leg at the resort and was recuperating in the Collingwood hospital. Fullerton was highly amused when Jozo dropped in, offered his condolences and asked for a loan. Actually, Jozo made it a regular practice to go to the hospital every Monday and visit anyone who had been injured during the weekend.

When Jozo's back was against the wall with his money problems, Senator Campbell was frequently there to help. Although the Senator's backing was a comfort, Jozo's situation was very tenuous. Until 1948 Blue Mountain Resorts did not have a secure mandate to run the ski operation. The original tows, trails, clubhouse and resort lands were owned by the organization that had been formed by the ski clubs: Blue Mountain Ski Club (1940) Inc. Blue Mountain Resorts had outright ownership of the Lodge and the nine-acre parcel on which it sat, but it had to make short-term arrangements from time to time to lease and manage the other 345 acres used for skiing. Every two years or so there would be a financial crisis with the clubs that Jozo would have to skate through. "I have taken over management of your Collingwood property," he wrote to the Toronto Ski Club in 1946. "I got a number of tows with antiquated motors, rusty pulleys and shredded ropes," he pointed out, explaining why things were so difficult. "I have received the trails into my care, some of them uncut for years." He outlined a four-year plan and set about the improvements that were necessary. It was dubbed "Uncle Joe's Four-Year Plan," after the Five-Year Plans of "Uncle Joe" Stalin and the Communists. Despite his brave words and plans he had to operate on a shoestring, and the improvements consisted mainly of putting up rope tows made out of war-surplus equipment, smoothing and widening the old trails, and cutting a few new ones, such as the Check and Double Check (the latter was nicknamed "Czech and Double Czech" by Len Meyer). That area is now known as the Rabbit's Run by those who ski Blue Mountain North.

In 1948, at a vitally important meeting of Blue Mountain Ski Club (1940) Inc., Jozo had to use all of his powers of persuasion and charm in an attempt to get a long-term lease for Blue Mountain Resorts from the ski clubs. He offered them an arrangement whereby, in return for a long lease, they could increase their share ownership in Blue Mountain Resorts Limited and retain perpetual skiing rights to the property. According to newspaper and eyewitness accounts, this was a stormy meeting, with considerable opposition to the deal that Jozo proposed. However, Jozo was able to persuade the meeting that he and his backer, Senator Campbell, were able to provide the leadership that was necessary for the successful development of the area. The agreement proposed by Jozo was supported by the most progressive of the leaders of the Blue Mountain and Toronto clubs. "We were determined that Blue Mountain should be developed as a public area," remembers Robert Gooch, who was a director of the TSC at the time. "Some of our group," he adds, "would have liked to have used this opportunity to secure the resort as a private club. Others among us didn't want the club to be involved in Collingwood at all." The most influential Collingwood ski official, John Smart, also backed the agreement and made the motion that the transaction be put into effect.

According to the agreement that was signed, the Toronto Ski Club received shares in Blue Mountain Resorts valued at $8,000, while the Blue Mountain Ski Club was paid $1,000 in cash. It apparently had been unable to equal the cash infusions that the TSC had been making. The clubs were guaranteed permanent skiing rights on the property. Blue Mountain Resorts emerged from the negotiations with one great advantage. The 1948 agreement provided for a 999-year lease on the resort lands. This enabled Blue Mountain Resorts to make long-term plans and to run its operations with a freer hand, although from time to time there had to be new negotiations with the Toronto Ski Club in accordance with the changing needs of both organizations. From a modern vantage point, some might regard this as a one-sided deal in favour of Blue Mountain Resorts. However, the ski operation at that time was losing money and needed visionaries like Jozo and Senator Campbell who were ready to make a total commitment to expanding the resort.

Having solidified his hold over the lands originally owned by the clubs, Jozo wasted no time in launching another ambitious undertaking. In 1948, just after he negotiated the long-term lease, he raised another $10,000, mainly by an $8,000 mortgage, and purchased the 150-acre Kinsey property immediately to the south of the main area. The Kinsey barn was converted into a Ski Barn, and the orchard on the Kinsey farm was partially cleared for ski operations. A rope tow powered by a Bren gun carrier was set up on the new slope, which was named the Apple Bowl. Jozo had commenced his two-mile march across the face of Blue Mountain.

Early arrivals checking in at the parking lot at the foot of Blue Mountain, c. 1954. On the second level of the Gatehouse was Jozo's command post, where he surveyed slopes with field glasses and issued instructions on his loudspeaker. Not shown in the photo were the gas pumps which were on the north side of the building. The real centre of activity was already the Ski Barn, further south, and the Gatehouse was eventually torn down. Also discontinued was the practice of charging a "guest fee" to skiers who were not members of the Toronto Ski Club or the Blue Mountain Ski Club. The fee was an irritation and caused a back-up of cars on the county road.

– Courtesy: Blue Mountain Resorts Limited, Credit: Jack Saunders

PART III

The 1950s: Barns, Downhills and Pots

The Fifties witnessed the southward expansion of the resort as Jozo opened up the new lands that he had purchased from the Kinsey family. The Ski Barn, with its rollicking parties, became the centre of activities, replacing the Lodge, which was sold to finance uphill transportation. Despite the changes many things around the resort remained the same; for example, there continued to be great interest in racing, especially on a dangerous new downhill trail, the Dieppe. Four-way skiing (slalom, downhill, cross-country and jumping) was dominated by the relentless Georgas brothers. Jozo continued to be harassed by financial pressures and had great difficulty in financing his first lift. He achieved his own rescue, however, when the discovery that the clay in the mountain was suitable for pottery sparked experiments that led to the development of a major business in ceramics.

From Gatehouse to Ski Barn

Toward the end of the 1940s, Jozo built a more elaborate entrance to the resort. Called the Gatehouse, the rambling structure demonstrated Jozo's inventiveness. It contained a ticket office for the collection of entrance fees and a larger building that housed a snack bar and administrative office. There were gas pumps, and Jozo exhorted skiers to fill their tanks before driving home. Each gallon bought, he pointed out, would bring the resort closer to the installation of a much-needed new lift. Above the ticket office was Jozo's command post, from where he could survey the northern slopes of the resort with a pair of field glasses. He installed a loudspeaker system that played music, which he would frequently interrupt with an announcement, a reprimand to a reckless skier or a summons to an employee. "You there in the red sweater," he would shout, "you're butting in; go to the end of the line. You in the blue jacket: slow down; you're skiing recklessly." His methods of dealing with parking offenders were equally heavy-handed. If a vehicle was in the way, Jozo might come along with his tractor and tow it into the ditch. No one enjoyed the surveillance, and the practice was discontinued after complaints were received. By 1949 the Ski Barn had been built, and it became increasingly active during the 1950s, replacing the Gatehouse as the centre of operations. The Gatehouse was eventually torn down.

Jozo was his own architect for the conversion of the Kinsey barn into a Ski Barn which housed overnight guests and served as the main entertainment centre and base lodge for the resort throughout the 1950s. The old beams, wooden floors, hanging wagon wheel and lanterns, and paintings by Walter Trier made for a totally original and charming atmosphere that is fondly remembered by those who skied Blue Mountain in the Fifties.

The new structure utilized the foundations and skeleton of the Kinsey barn. The cedar log technique that Jozo devised for the walls was probably inspired by something he had seen in Europe. It served his purposes, as he was always ready to improvise in order to take advantage of materials that were handy, in order to cut the cost of construction. Cedar rails from old fences on the Kinsey farm were cut up into foot-long lengths and mortared in between the barn's original beam work. Sawing up these rails on a farmer's buzz saw took hundreds of hours. The Ski Barn was renovated several times, and the ends of the logs were eventually stuccoed over. Originally they were uncovered and visible, adding to the rustic effect. At the north end of what had been the haymow, a large fireplace was set out from the wall. Above the mantelpiece was a humorous mural of square dancers, painted by Walter Trier. Along the walls were a series of cartoon-like paintings of prize-winning cows, also by Trier. From the ceiling hung a huge wagon wheel, painted yellow and equipped with lantern bulbs that illuminated a small hardwood dance floor. On the second level a series of dormitory-type rooms replaced the old granary bins and the loft. The rooms were laid out to front on a U-shaped corridor, with a railing to prevent the guests from falling down into the open area and dance floor below.

The Ski Barn was the scene of many après-ski parties. Jozo played the accordion and led singsongs, and there were also square dances. On these occasions the whole structure vibrated from the activity. Jozo was not always available to organize the entertainment, as he had so many other tasks, including ordering the weekly food supply, laying out new trails, and devising new schemes to finance the struggling resort and the emerging pottery business. On nights when he was busy, there would be a movie of the 1948 Olympics, occasioning a groan from the guests, as most had seen it many times before; or the P.A. system would be used to

The Ski Barn c. 1954, with the Ski Shop in background. This photo reveals the ends of the cedar logs used in the construction. Later they were stuccoed over.
– Courtesy: Jack MacMurchy, Credit: Jack Saunders

Jozo Weider at the Ski Barn, c. 1949.
– Courtesy: Blue Mountain

The Ski Barn's famous homemade pie, 15 cents, c. 1949.
Left to right: Les Tucker, Wearie Williams and Ede Williams.
– Courtesy: Sue Boehm, Credit: Les Tucker

Skiers join in après-ski party singsong led by Wearie Williams, Jozo Weider on accordion and Peter Kingsmill, c. 1949. – Courtesy: Jack MacMurchy

Walter Trier's mural above the fireplace graces the scene of one of the many social functions held in the Ski Barn, c. 1951.
– Courtesy: Blue Mountain Resorts Limited

The Blue Mountain Ski Shop, c. 1953. The loft had been added to the former sheep barn, using Jozo's cedar log construction method.
– Courtesy: Jack MacMurchy, Credit: Les Tucker

play scratchy Glen Miller records, and young men from the surrounding chalets, nattily attired in black Irving ski pants, would compete for the Michigan girls staying at the Barn. Seldom did the partying go beyond midnight, as Jozo insisted that his guests retire and get a good night's sleep in order to be fresh for the next day's skiing. Jozo was a strict chaperone, protecting his single female guests at the Lodge and Ski Barn against predatory male skiers. His concern is remembered today with gratitude by many who are now mothers or grandmothers, but he must have let down his vigilance on at least one occasion. In 1985 a telephone call was received from a woman who wanted the guest list for the New Year's Eve party of 1956. When pressed for the reason, she replied that she believed that she had been conceived that night, and she was now searching for her father.

Beside the Ski Barn was an old sheep barn that Jozo converted into a ski shop. The main section was within the original square-timbered walls, but a loft was added, using the same technique employed in the construction of the Ski Barn. Cedar logs, about 12 inches in length, were mortared around the upper windows to form the wall above the log section. The shop was operated by Jozo's wife, Helen, who sold her own hand-knitted "Weidermade" sweaters and mitts. In the fall the building was used to store apples picked in the orchards between the Ski Barn and the Apple Bowl.

The ski shop also served as a centre of the Blue Mountain Ski School, which was a very tiny one at the time. In the mid-1950s the principal instructor was a lanky former Austrian racer named Henri Moser. He had excellent technical ability and occasionally coached my sister Helen and me. We were racing at the time. We considered ourselves lucky to sandwich our runs between the jobs assigned to us by Jozo, on the family farm, the resort and in the new pottery business. We were glad when Jozo, by popular request, disconnected his loudspeaker at the Gatehouse, which meant that he could not continue to publicly hail us and instruct us to report to the Ski Barn for dishwashing.

Helen Weider dominated junior racing in Ontario during the 1950s and also won many senior competitions. In 1954, after sweeping various provincial meets, she won the first of two back-to-back Canadian Junior Alpine titles. Injuries and Jozo's concern for her studies made her decline invitations to try out for the Olympic team. I did well in 1955, winning the Ontario Junior Downhill and a bronze medal in the Canadian Junior Slalom. I soon learned ski-jumping and cross-country, travelling to Nordic meets with Jim and Bill Georgas. I entered my first race on a pair

Helen Weider powers through a slalom course, c. 1955. She dominated Ontario women's racing in the 1950s and won two Canadian Junior Alpine Championships. – Courtesy: Charles Garrad

University of Toronto "Ski Blues" 1956-57. Left to right, rear: J. Hethrington (Manager), J. R. Britton, J. A. Ronback, A. Poutanen, S. S. Swenson. Left to right, front: G. Weider, W. M. McIntyre, W. G. Beck (Coach), D. W. Esson, D. C. Palmateer. Absent: M. H. McLeod.
– Courtesy: University of Toronto Archive "A79-0060"

of cross-country skis that were crafted in the basement of the Ski Barn by Jozo, who used a ripsaw to narrow down an old pair of slalom skis that someone had left behind. Jozo had enjoyed the Nordic sports in his native country and dreamed of making Blue Mountain an international ski-jumping centre. When he was ready to activate the first of two jumps that he built, he drove excitedly into Collingwood, summoned me out of my high school class and took me to try out the jump to see if it would work.

I entered the University of Toronto at age 18, and my four-way talents earned me a place on the ski team. The U of T skiers had a long tradition at Blue Mountain, dating back to the early 1940s. The ski team used a cabin near the bottom of the Happy Valley, and at one point they had attempted to build a ski jump above the cabin, on the steep ridge opposite the Hog's Back, on the southern side. Throughout the Fifties the team's coach was Bill Beck, who had been a top Ontario racer and who was active in the administration of the Toronto Ski Club. In February 1957 Beck and the ski team were jubilant when they won the Quebec-Ontario intercollegiate championship, breaking the monopoly that had been enjoyed by McGill. The competition was held at Blue Mountain, and some of the trophies were made in Jozo's new pottery which he was getting underway. It was a short trip for the trophy mugs from the kilns in the basement of the Ski Barn to the main area upstairs where they were presented.

The resort had two good downhill trails, the Kandahar and the Dieppe. The Dieppe was particularly difficult. Near the end of the 1940s, Bob Gooch, Bill Beck and other racing enthusiasts with the Toronto Ski Club and the University of Toronto wanted to have a downhill course as demanding as those in the Laurentians, in order to host top-level competitions. They thought the Kandahar was too easy, especially after it had been widened by Jozo. Using axes and crosscut saws, Beck and other volunteers carved out a new trail that forked off from the Kandahar into steep ravines and deep gullies at northern edge of the resort. It began on top of the cornice on the Back 40s and terminated just behind the Blue Mountain Lodge. It was called the Dieppe, after the disastrous World War II beachhead; the name turned out to be appropriate in view of the many casualties claimed by the run before it was phased out in the Sixties.

The downhillers who braved the Dieppe had to hold their edges on a treacherous fade-away corner and plummet down a steep pitch called

Cutting the Dieppe, 1948. Left to right: Bill Beck, David Cochran, Tony Kingsmill and Burny Clark. The stumps were dynamited out by Bob Gooch. He aroused the wrath of neighbouring farmers for blasting on Sundays. They remembered the incident and punished the resort when the liquor vote came around. – Courtesy: David Cochran

"The Dive." Reaching top speed on the "The Dive," they immediately entered a tight, twisting "S" turn followed by a plunge into a jarring gully. As the trail was only 25 feet wide in places, there was little margin for error. It was considered cowardly to wear protective headgear. Skilled racers who refrained from checking covered the three-quarters of a mile in less than a minute.

When the Canadian Alpine Championships were held on the Schuss and Dieppe in 1955, the Dieppe was mastered by the top amateur and professional racers in the country. The perennial Peter Kingsmill, who had joined Osler, was back at his old haunts, the Blue Mountain Lodge, organizing the event. Several hundred spectators lined the course, shielding themselves behind trees to watch the daredevil contestants. The conditions were lightning fast on the hard, icy course, and the hill record was broken again and again that day. It was shaved down to 54 seconds, never to be bettered, in a courageous dash by Henri Moser, who also won the professional category in slalom against a talented field. Among the amateurs, the Alpine combined winner was John Clifford from Ottawa. He was a member of a famous skiing family and played a pioneering role in the development of Camp Fortune. Clifford would later make an important contribution to Blue Mountain by introducing the resort to the Great Slide Ride.

Rick Marshall mastering the Dieppe to win the Central Canadian Championship in 1950. – Courtesy: David Cochran

Jim Georgas on the Barn Hill, 1947.
– Courtesy: Jim Georgas

Bill Georgas at the foot of Blue Mountain, 1951.
– Courtesy: Jack MacMurchy, Credit: D. O. Deacon

Earl Georgas, affectionately known as "Uncle Merle," was awarded Toronto Ski Club's Julian Sale Trophy in 1983 for his dedication in introducing over 500 children to the joys of skiing.
– Courtesy: Blue Mountain Resorts Limited

The greatest four-way competitors in Ontario were Bill and Jim Georgas. They were born and raised in Owen Sound, where their Greek immigrant parents operated small businesses and raised a family of 10 children. Four of them – Louis, Bill, Jim and Earl – have amassed an unparalleled record of skiing honours and accomplishments that spans the entire 50-year history of Blue Mountain. Louis, the second-eldest, competed in the very first ski meet held at Blue Mountain, in the winter of 1938. A self-taught wizard on skis, he was only 19 the following year when he won a sensational victory in slalom at the Dominion Ski Championships at Fort William, defeating the famous Norwegian ski jumper and all-around competitor Reider Anderson and Canadian four-way champion Punch Blott.

Jim and Bill Georgas dominated Ontario racing throughout the Fifties, competing in all four events in one exhausting weekend after another. As well as regularly winning provincial championships in downhill and slalom, Jim Georgas was almost as successful in the Nordic events. With the determination and thoroughness that characterized his approach to training, he went to Sudbury and Sault Ste. Marie and spent three months studying the waxing and racing techniques of the Finns. He soon began chasing and frequently beating his former teachers. His relentless consistency in every type of competition won him repeated Ontario four-way championships during the 1950s. Bill Georgas was always hard on Jim's heels. He was almost as proficient in the four-way test and sometimes edged Jim out in Alpine events. The best that most other competitors could usually hope for was third place.

Some of the Nordic competitions were held at Blue Mountain, but the ski jump that Jozo built at the south edge of the Apple Bowl was only about 25 metres and more suitable for training than for top-level competition. A larger jump had been built at Midland by Pete Pettersen, an immigrant from Norway who had settled there after training at Camp Borden with the Norwegian Air Force during the war. The Georgas brothers trained with Pettersen, became ski jumpers and soon began pressing the Finns in that event. Onlookers at a provincial competition on Midland's jumping hill were horrified when one of Bill Georgas's skis came off in mid-flight. He came down uninjured in a spectacular crash landing. Bill was less fortunate when he slammed into a tree at high speed and broke his leg near the bottom of Dieppe while practising for the Canadian Championships in 1955. He was splinted and then carted off to the hospital by Jozo, who had heard his cry of pain from nearby Blue Mountain Lodge.

The Georgas Team entry in the 1988 Todd Brooker Ski Challenge. Left to right: Ron Lombard, Jim Georgas, Bill Georgas and Earl Georgas.
– Courtesy: Jim Georgas, Credit: Kodak Canada

In 1954 the Georgas brothers led a miraculous rescue effort at Blue Mountain when a skier was reported missing at the end of a Sunday afternoon. Jozo organized the search, and the five-man search party probed through heavy snowdrifts near the top of the mountain while a howling snowstorm raged around them. Breaking trail a few steps ahead of the rest of the party, Bill Georgas was amazed to hear a faint voice, which turned out to be that of George Bornet, the lost skier. He had gone touring by himself and had been buried in a creek bed for five hours by an avalanche which had been caused by the collapse of a cornice of heavy snow. A narrow crack in the six-foot mass of snow allowed Bornet to breathe, to see the rays of Bill Georgas's flashlight and to be heard when he shouted for help. Using their hands, sticks and tree branches, the rescuers spent two hours digging Bornet out of the tomb of snow and icy water that had encased him. Then they carried him down to the Ski Barn, where he was warmed up and dispatched to the Collingwood hospital. Handcrafted plaques were inscribed by Bornet after he had recovered, and these were sent to each member of the search party. Bill Georgas values Bornet's plaque more than the hundreds of ski trophies that he has accumulated over the years.

The fourth Georgas brother, Earl, specialized in ski instruction; he taught hundreds of tiny skiers at the Toronto Ski Club and was awarded the Julian Sale trophy for his efforts.

Jim Georgas's racing career never really ended. In 1988 he swept all events in his age group in the Canadian National Masters Championship at Whistler, British Columbia, and the following year won gold and bronze medals in the World Masters at Sun Valley, Idaho.

The spectacular racing events of the 1950s raised the profile of the resort, and the Ski Barn was very popular with visitors, but Jozo continued to be pressed by financial problems. There were many sleepless nights during which he twisted and turned while trying to figure out how to keep his creditors at bay. In the first 10 years of the resort's operation, expenditures were frequently greater than revenues. The 1950 tax return, for example, shows that the resort lost $12,500 that year. Not only was Jozo financially strapped in relation to the resort's requirements for expansion, but he was hardly able to support his family. In the early Fifties he took summer jobs, putting in two summers as the manager of the Caledon Trout Club and spending another one operating a food pavilion and dance hall on Lake Couchiching at Orillia. The first endeavour was a successful one, allowing him to make many contacts among wealthy businessmen in the fishing club; the second was a disaster. He lost money on the food concession, and he and I were beaten up by some toughs when we tried to expel them from a dance.

Capitalizing the resort's first lift, the pomalift (later called the North Pomalift), built in 1955, was a complex affair requiring some sleight-of-hand financing and a multi-tiered scheme of ticket prices to cope with discounts required by the Toronto Ski Club. In 1951 Jozo had been compelled to sell the Lodge to the club for $15,000 to retire that amount in loans that the club had advanced. In 1955 the club in turn sold the Lodge for $20,000 in order to help the resort finance the construction of the pomalift, for which around $30,000 was needed. Some additional capital was also required for the trail network around the new lift. The club now loaned the company $18,000, which was secured by a mortgage on the pomalift and a second mortgage on the whole ski area. Jozo raised another $15,000 with a public issue of convertible debentures, which diluted his equity in the company and entangled him in a snarl of red tape as a result of securities regulations.

To ensure a sufficient flow of funds, skiers were invited to subscribe for pomalift tickets in advance of the season at a 40-percent discount; the full rate was set at 50 cents a ride. At least $10,000 worth of tickets had to be sold on subscription before construction of the lift could begin. The Toronto Ski Club was a major subscriber and sold the advance tickets to its members. The subscribers paid 30 cents per single-ride ticket (there were no day passes for the lift) while members of the TSC who did not

The north area, fall 1955, prior to the opening of the pomalift which was under construction, the towers being visible. The Spectacular had been cleared, but the area on both sides of the lift line between the Schuss and the Spectacular was tree-covered. The log clubhouse was still on the property but was removed shortly afterward. The Red Devil had been removed.
– Courtesy: Collingwood Museum

During the winter of 1953-54, Jozo implored skiers to assist with the financing of the proposed T-bar (a pomalift was constructed). WE NEED YOUR SUPPORT SKIERS . . . *See Jozo Today!"*
– Courtesy: Jack Saunders, Credit: Jack Saunders

subscribe still enjoyed a discount of 20 percent and paid 40 cents per ticket. The 20-percent discount was to remain in effect until the TSC mortgage was paid off. The price to the general public was 50 cents. The tickets were printed in strips perforated into three coupons, and a different colour was used for each of the three categories. One full strip was required for a ride on the pomalift, while a ride on one of the rope tows could be had for one coupon.

Although rates were raised as a result of the use of single-ride tickets on the pomalift, they remained quite reasonable. Those who did not want to buy the pomalift tickets at 30 to 50 cents per ride could use the eight rope tows for only $2 a day. Jozo was very annoyed with the complex rate schedules imposed by the TSC's conditions, and not a patient man under any circumstances, he frequently exploded with rage during meetings with club directors concerning this and other subjects. In spite of the clashes the directors treated Jozo affectionately, presenting him with an accordion at one of the TSC's gala celebrations. (After Jozo's death the TSC named a room in the clubhouse after him, where his portrait was hung, and established an award in his honour.) It was not until 1968 that Jozo was able to pay off the mortgage and get rid of the 20-percent discount, although a 10-percent discount still had to be paid as a result of earlier agreements. In 1971 he negotiated a more reasonable agreement

The North Poma officially opened in December 1955. The first such lift to be installed in Canada, it replaced the old central rope tow and the Red Devil to become the main uphill transportation for the resort. In addition to appearing at openings such as this one, Reeve D. J. McNichol supplied poles for Jozo's rope tow. He was dismayed when he had to wait several months to get paid. Left to right: Jozo Weider, Reeve Dave McNichol, Ken Skelton.
– Courtesy: Jack MacMurchy, Credit: Herb Hall

with the TSC which eliminated some of the complexities that had been so vexing.

The original subscribers' tickets for the North Pomalift, usually referred to as "red tickets," have become collectors' items, framed by some families and hung on the walls of their chalets. Occasionally they are presented, as a joke, to puzzled lift operators in lieu of the regular day or season pass.

The pomalift, which was installed along the route of the old Grand Central rope tow, was strongly welcomed by Blue Mountain skiers, who were glad to find something new after 18 years on the rope tows and the Red Devil. They also enjoyed the new trails that were opened along with

Skiers anxiously await a ride on Blue Mountain's first pomalift.
– Courtesy: Jack MacMurchy

Welcoming the pomalift, 1955. This photo appeared in the December 12, 1955, edition of the Toronto Star: *"Loaded with equipment for the finest of Sunday sports, say they, are Betty Garratt, Joan Lister and Pat Wooller, who tried the slopes near Collingwood yesterday, await the lift which will go into operation at the hills next week."* – Courtesy: Joe Williams, Credit: *Toronto Star*

the lift in 1955. The Schuss had been lengthened and rerouted so that it could be accessed from the upper terminal of the pomalift, and the imposing Spectacular had been cut on the south side of the lift line. The Senator, which had been cut in 1948 and named after Senator Campbell, was extended and connected to the Spectacular so that the more cautious skiers could circumnavigate the upper pitches of what was then, and has remained, the steepest run on the mountain. The installation of the pomalift meant the end of the Red Devil, which was dismantled, and another monument of the Blue Mountain Ski Club, the log clubhouse, was also removed from the premises.

Pomalifts, or pomas as they were sometimes called, became widely used at the resort during the 1960s, after the North Poma was successfully introduced. Another pomalift was built in 1962, this one on the Apple Bowl, and more followed. The device was the invention of French engineering genius Jean Pomagalski. In some respects it was superior to T-bars, which Jozo had also been considering. The main advantage was that it allowed a single rider to be towed up the hill, while on a T-bar, each skier was paired with another and had to ski up in balance with his neighbour. The Pomagalski factory in Grenoble later became a supplier of chairlifts as well as pomas to the resort.

The very success of the North Pomalift created a problem, as the new lift immediately suffered long line-ups. Impatient skiers had already started one private club (Osler) partly to get away from the crowds. It was clear that Jozo would have to keep pushing forward with the expansion programs that he found so difficult to finance. The pressures were acute, but the greater the adversity, the more magic Jozo seemed to be able to work. This time his creative solution consisted of digging up a piece of Blue Mountain, baking it in the Ski Barn and selling it to the world.

Pottery glazers busy at work in the Ski Barn, c. 1953.
– Courtesy: Mike & Mary Jaroch, Credit: Herb Hall

Pottery Saves a Resort

At the beginning of the 1950s, Jozo began experimenting with pottery-making in the basement of the Ski Barn. He hit upon the idea when he found out that Denis Tupy, a Czechoslovakian immigrant who was working as a dishwasher in the kitchen of the Ski Barn, had some training in pottery in his native country and knew how to make plaster moulds that could be used in production of clay vases and figurines. Setting out to learn everything he could about the process, Jozo spent long evenings poring over technical manuals. He and Tupy built several kilns out of fire-brick and began production on a modest scale. They utilized the clay that was dug up by bulldozers when trails were being prepared at the resort. The early operation was a small one, not much more than a hobby. Courses in pottery-making were taught in the Ski Barn as part of an arts and crafts program that Jozo had introduced in order to attract summer guests. Soon, however, Jozo began to appreciate the commercial potential and he increased the scope of the business.

Starting up the pottery was hard work for Jozo and his family. The clay had to be gathered, aged and mixed. Moulds had to be prepared and set out in a crude version of an assembly line. The liquefied clay was poured into the moulds until set, then the pots were carefully removed from the moulds and manually scraped and smoothed by workers with knives and sponges. Two firings followed, the first for the raw pottery, the second

An early piece of Blue Mountain pottery takes shape out of local clay on Jozo Weider's potter's wheel, c. 1953. – Courtesy: Mike & Mary Jaroch

after a glaze had been applied. The original kilns were not automated and had to be manually controlled. In each kiln there was a peephole through which one would look at a ceramic cone inside the kiln. When the pots were sufficiently cooked or glazed, the cone would be bent and the kiln turned off. Sometimes a worker would forget to check on the cone and turn off the kiln, which consequently would be destroyed by a molten mass of glaze and clay. The lava would coat the bricks and could not be scraped off. The next day Jozo would be found building a new kiln, ripping out the ruined bricks and electrical elements, and replacing them with new ones. This was unpleasant work, as handling the firebricks caused cuts and abrasions on the fingers, and the gritty brick dust flew into one's eyes. Packing and shipping was a major ordeal as well, because of the cramped conditions in the Ski Barn. One of the most popular figurines was a swan with a long, slender neck. Each swan had to be splinted with cardboard at the neck before being wrapped in tissue and an outer layer of newspaper like the other items.

Blue Mountain Pottery began to catch on almost immediately. The graceful vases, dishes and figurines were glazed in attractive brown, green, blue and orange hues. When fired at high heat the glazes ran together and produced a variegated colour pattern; the deep, rich green was the most favoured. Because the glazes dripped and ran together under heat, no two pieces were exactly the same. The fact that the pottery was made at Blue Mountain from local clay enhanced the appeal, and Jozo used his promotional skills and showmanship to good advantage. Upon learning to use the potter's wheel he demonstrated the art of hand-turning whenever the opportunity occurred. He was proud of the toughness and durability of his pots, and in moments of enthusiasm, he would drop one to the floor to demonstrate its strength. While the test was usually successful, it occasionally failed, and onlookers would be amused when a piece broke into smithereens on reaching the ground.

Jozo was encouraged by the quick acceptance of his pottery and opened a larger production centre combined with a retail outlet on Highway 26. He soon began to get orders from major department stores. If necessary he would bring a bushel of apples from the resort's orchards or a load of firewood to help persuade a Simpsons buyer to take on the new, untried product. The expansion continued and an export market developed, with sales to the United States, Great Britain and Australia.

Jozo's speed, decisiveness and ability to improvise was a great asset in his efforts to increase production. When he heard about a pottery in the Ohio Valley that had failed and closed its doors, he went there and bought everything inside the building at a bargain price. He stayed three weeks, dismantling the factory with the help of its former employees. In anticipation he had rented a former aircraft parts factory on Pine Street in Collingwood, and here he trucked kilns, moulds and clay-mixing equipment from Ohio, establishing a large-scale operation at the Pine Street plant. In 1960 he made yet another move, building a brand-new factory and retail outlet on the western edge of Collingwood.

Those who worked at the pottery found Jozo to be a fun-loving but unpredictable boss. Employees had to be ready for any assignment. There were several uprooted Czechoslovakians in key positions, including Mike Jaroch and Denis Tupy. Jaroch had fled Czechoslovakia in 1949 and arrived in Canada penniless and unable to speak any English. Until he was able to learn English in night school, the only job he could get was looking after chickens. He was hired by Jozo in 1954 and was given diverse assignments in both the resort and the pottery businesses. As well as holding down a regular job in the pottery, he was on hand as the resort's only ski instructor during the week. When a guest of the resort requested a ski lesson, Mike had to do a quick change into ski clothing

Following removal from the mold, Susan Chastven trims and smoothes this piece of pottery, c. 1963. – Courtesy: Blue Mountain Resorts Limited

By 1963 Blue Mountain Pottery had gone into mass production.
– Courtesy: Blue Mountain Resorts

and rush out to the hill. Mike spent more than 25 years with the Blue Mountain Ski School and the Canadian Ski Instructors' Alliance, putting legions of skiers through their paces in his jovial Czech accent. He also endured through hundreds of après-ski parties at Blue Mountain Lodge, the Ski Barn, and later the Blue Mountain Inn.

The pottery was a wonderful business, generating outstanding retail sales to tourists in Collingwood, as well as developing solid domestic and foreign markets. Even the "seconds," or slightly-flawed pieces, found ready buyers when offered at a discount at the Collingwood outlet. Demand for the "seconds" was so pronounced that they threatened to eat into sales of the regular product, and Jozo jokingly considered converting the whole operation to manufacture the second-rate goods. The consistent revenues and profits from the new venture gave Jozo a safety net for the shaky and seasonal ski business and at last produced a decent income for his family. Blue Mountain Pottery was Jozo's most creative achievement. It was also the turning point in his business career, rescuing him from the brink of failure and assuring his success as a businessman.

Susan Waters and Anna Weider ride the South Chair during the official opening ceremonies on January 18, 1960.
– Courtesy: Blue Mountain Resorts Limited

The standing rock at the Scenic Caves, called Ekarenniondi *by the Petun Indian tribe, which maintained villages on the escarpment in the 16th and 17th centuries. The Caves were a short walk from the new South Chair. An important tourist attraction, they are owned at present by Toronto-Collingwood entrepreneur Terry Rodgers.* – Courtesy: Collingwood Museum

PART IV

The 1960s: The Resort Modernizes

The Sixties were an era of expansion. Jozo rose to the challenge of the new ski clubs that were flanking the resort along the escarpment and began to modernize aggressively. While Blue Mountain's financial picture had improved as a result of the success of Blue Mountain Pottery, Jozo continued to be plagued by a problem that had bothered him from the day that he arrived at Blue Mountain: the failure to get a liquor licence for his base lodge and dining room. As the flow of skiers swelled, the town of Collingwood became increasingly interested in the sport and began to be recognized as "the Ski Capital of Ontario." Near the north end of the resort, a village of shacks had risen during the Fifties; the resort community was now enlarged by more extensive development as new clusters of chalets took shape in the lee of the mountain. At the close of the Sixties Jozo was near the end of his life and could look back on an impressive career as an entrepreneur and industrialist.

New Lifts, New Runs

In 1960 John F. Kennedy was elected President of the United States and immediately began a race to catch up with Soviet space technology and put a man on the moon. At Blue Mountain Jozo also had technology on his agenda as he rushed to introduce modern machinery and buildings to compete with Georgian Peaks, private ski clubs and other new resorts that were springing up in Southern Ontario. It was a time when improvements were being demanded by the market, but most importantly, the market was strong. Jozo's predictions were starting to come true. North Americans were turning to leisure pursuits with increasing alacrity. As a result of the strong economic conditions of the Sixties they had bigger discretionary incomes and were spending heavily on recreation. Skiing fitted well into the affluent new culture, especially with the advances made in equipment. In the United States the design engineer Howard Head, adapting materials from the aircraft industry, had come up with a metal ski that weighed about a third less than the regular wooden models. He had started out with six employees and produced 300 pairs of skis in 1950. He took the Head Ski Company public in 1960, and five years later was selling 100,000 pairs annually with revenues of $9 million.

The new Head Standards were lively and easy to handle. After being perfected by Head, they did not crack, and they turned easily without shimmying and clattering. They also required almost no maintenance. The first Head ski was the beginning of a tide of innovations with fibreglass and metal by Head and other manufacturers. To complete the revolution in equipment there were buckle boots and safety bindings. The Salomon "step-in" binding available in 1966 made it almost effortless to get into one's skis. Ski resort operators started widening their slopes and using grooming vehicles to pack them. Not only was it easier to ski because of the equipment and the improved trails, but it was easier to get to Blue Mountain. Train travel to Collingwood had dwindled to almost nothing by the end of the 1950s, and no regular passenger trains ran in the 1960s, although the ski trains were revived for two seasons. But the decline was primarily because skiers found it faster and more convenient to use cars and buses, especially after Highway 400 was opened in the early 1950s. The roads to the mountain from Highway 26 had been widened and improved, and snow plowing had become increasingly routine.

All of these changes added up to a major opportunity for Jozo, and he set out to drive the resort ahead as it had never been driven before. He had anticipated the trend and had made his third key land acquisition in 1958, the 200-acre Plater farm between the O-Hill and the Apple Bowl. He now set out to develop up all of his southern and central territory. The decade of modernity was launched on January 18, 1960, with the opening of the South Chair between the O-Hill and the L-Hill. This double chairlift was the first chairlift in Ontario. Jozo was proud that the chairs were 80 feet in the air at the highest point and used this fact in advertisements. In addition to transporting skiers, the lift was used to carry summer visitors to the top of the escarpment. After arriving at the top, they could visit the nearby Scenic Caves. A restaurant, the Höhenblick Café, was built near the top terminal. It afforded a fine view of Georgian Bay and the Collingwood harbour.

Jozo's new chairlift was followed by a stream of additional improvements. In 1965 he built a second double chairlift, the North Chair beside the pomalift. Two more double chairlifts, Tranquility and Apple Bowl, were added in 1969. A fifth double chairlift was built on the O-Hill in 1971, shortly before Jozo's death. The five chairlifts installed by Jozo represented an investment of almost $600,000. Another $350,000

At left: *A great deal of history is contained in this 1971 photo of the north-central part of the resort. The Happy Valley, to the left of the heavily moguled Hog's Back, was a widened version of the old Lumber Trail. The steep and narrow trail perpendicular to the Happy Valley was called the Instructors' Run in the 1960s but had once been the path of a ski jump built by University of Toronto skiers. The Hog's Back, now a Blue Mountain trail, had been the site of Ross Wilson's Happy Valley rope tow, which he had operated in 1947-48. A return to the north from the Happy Valley was allowed by a gap in the tree line, or skiers could continue down to the Ski Barn and the lifts there. The Barn is not visible in this photo, but it does contain the original Kinsey farmhouse, which was used as a staff house for employees of the resort. Below the staff house and on the other side of the road was the barn of the farm owned by Gordon Campbell, great-grandson of the original settler. He was employed by Jozo's resort and pottery businesses during the 1950s. Gordon's father, Charlie Campbell, had gradually sold off pieces of his farm, and some of the oldest chalets at Blue Mountain were located on these lots. In the centre of a ribbon of houses on the mountainside was a large house built by Jozo for artist Walter Trier in 1949. The highest building on the mountainside was the Youth Hostel, built in 1956. The cabin immediately beside the Hostel had been the base facility of the Happy Valley resort.*
– Courtesy: Blue Mountain Resorts Limited, Credit: Fritz Schuller

was spent on two modern buildings, the Blue Mountain Inn (1963) and the Central Base Lodge (1969). A six-acre lake had been bulldozed in the central area of the resort and was used to support a snowmaking system on the Apple Bowl. The improvements were financed by loans from the Bank of Commerce and the Industrial Development Bank, a $100,000 debenture issue, reinvestment of earnings, and cash infusions from Jozo's other businesses.

Along with lift construction came trail preparation. The hayfields on the Kinsey and Plater farms were already open, but they had to be reshaped in some places and connected by trails to the terminals of the new lifts. During most summers in the Sixties the mountain reverberated with the noise of chain saws and bulldozers. Although there were heavy earth-moving machines to root out the stumps and shape the ground, a good deal of manual labour was still required. "Picking stones is all we seemed to be doing every summer," recalls Larry Plater, who was working outdoors at the time. The soil bed above the shale underlay was full of rocks that had to be hauled away. The lumps of heavy clay that had been churned up by the bulldozers and then hardened by their tracks had to be raked smooth and seeded. Digging the foundations for the lift towers was back-breaking work. The holes for the South Chair were eight-feet square and eight-feet deep. They had to be dug with pick and shovel through the clay, shale and other rock.

View of the Apple Bowl, c. 1965. The Apple Bowl was served by a pomalift and double chair. The chair was the third chairlift at Blue Mountain and was built in 1969. The Greening T-Bar in the centre of the area supplemented the chair, and a pomalift served the easier slope above the Ski Barn. The 20-room Blue Mountain Inn was built in 1963, replacing the Ski Barn as an accommodations centre.
– Courtesy: Bill & Sue Skelton, Credit: Fritz Schuller

The result of this work made the effort worthwhile. At the end of nearly 11 years of modernization by Jozo, skiers had a swift ride up the mountain and an unprecedented variety of runs available to them. In 1971 the five chairlifts, supplemented by four pomalifts, three T-bars and one rope tow, allowed the resort to comfortably handle as many as 3,600 skiers in a day. Jozo's showpiece run opened in 1969, and his choice of a name was an inspired one. He called it Tranquility, after the great lunar sea that was being explored by the astronauts that year. Blue Mountain's Tranquility became an instant hit; its consistent vertical drop and smoothly rolling pitches made it the favourite cruise on the mountain. There were other fine new runs: Smart Alec, named after Jozo's first grandson; the lower Big Baby for beginners; the upper reaches of the O-Hill; Calamity Lane beside the new Greening T-bar on the north side of the Apple Bowl; and at the north, the Hog's Back and a definitively widened Happy Valley. Improvements were made to the Kandahar and trails between the Schuss and the North Chair lift line.

A major feature of the resort since Jozo's modernization efforts has been the opportunity of making one's way from one end of the mountain

Jozo, the businessman. While the prevalent image of Jozo was that of the wild man of the hills, he could hold his own on Bay Street when he dressed in a smart-looking business suit, or "borrowing clothes" as the local farmers knowingly commented when they saw him heading for Toronto in this attire. Controlling his accent, he could be suave and impressive in business presentations. This formal photo was taken by Ashley and Crippen c. 1960.
– Courtesy: Blue Mountain Resorts Limited, Credit: Ashley & Crippen

Jozo and his managers, 1969. Left to right: Ernie McCulloch, Jozo Weider, Leo Low, Bill Skelton and Gerry Baker.
– Courtesy: Blue Mountain Resorts Limited, Credit: Fritz Schuller

Tribute to Senator Campbell. In the 1960s Jozo used the name Blue Mountain Winter Park. It was changed to Blue Mountain Park at the end of the decade to emphasize the year-round nature of the resort. After Jozo's death, the word Park was dropped, and the operation was referred to as Blue Mountain Resorts or simply Blue Mountain. Some skiers have shortened it even further to "Blue."
– Courtesy: Blue Mountain Resorts Limited, Credit: Fritz Schuller

to the other, encountering a wide variety of trails and slopes. Jozo advertised this in his slogan, "The vertical drop is three miles wide." He was exaggerating by a mile, but his pride was pardonable. This type of breadth was unique among Ontario resorts and demonstrated Jozo's courage and foresight in amassing more than 800 acres of escarpment land. Of all the slopes, the Apple Bowl was the most popular. It had been sculpted out of the orchards and fields farmed by Arthur Kinsey, and then by Jozo. As each widening took place, more fruit trees were removed, and none remained when the slope was photographed in 1965. The north side of the Apple Bowl was served by the Greening T-bar, immediately in front of the new Blue Mountain Inn. The 20-room Inn had replaced the Ski Barn as the resort's accommodations centre. The aging Ski Barn was used for special functions in connection with races and group visits until it was torn down in 1978 in anticipation of the Chateau Ridge condominiums, which were built on that site during the 1980s.

Along with the expansion program, Jozo turned the corner from one-man entrepreneurship to modern management, recruiting a strong team of executives to run the various departments of the operation. Leo Low, an urbane and efficient Viennese hotel specialist, came from Mt. Tremblant to take over financial affairs and general administration. Low made an important contribution to the modernization of the resort by organizing the operation into departments and establishing systematic financial controls. He was also successful in negotiating loans totalling more than $1 million, which were used to fuel the resort's expansion under Jozo's successors. Also recruited by Jozo from Mt. Tremblant at about the same time was Ernie McCulloch, who took over the ski school and ski shop. His name was very prominent in skiing circles and brought prestige to the resort. Gerry Baker was induced to come to Blue Mountain from Toronto to take over advertising and promotion. He built a chalet on property obtained from Jozo above the Ski Barn and the Walter Trier house, where he settled permanently with his wife, Joanne, and his daughters, Andrea and Karen. The girls became championship ski racers. After leaving the resort's employ in 1973, Baker remained in the area and later became publisher of a popular local magazine.

Two natives of the area started in humble positions and worked their way up the administrative ladder. Harold Abbotts' first job was serving hotdogs at the Ski Barn. He later moved into accounting and eventually succeeded Leo Low as Vice-President of Finance. He persevered through eye-blearing number-crunching and grinding correspondence courses to win the top financial position. Bill Skelton was the area manager in the 1960s and was appointed Vice-President of Operations after Jozo's death. Skelton, who as a teenager had worked on machines under the guidance of his father, Ken, played a key role in the expansion of Blue Mountain, contributing management skills and strong technical knowledge of trail

Jozo and Senator Campbell at Craigleith Station, 1944. Campbell was a director of several major corporations and was counsel to Collingwood Terminals, headed by Norman Boadway. In addition to backing Jozo Weider, he was a friend of Collingwood, donating to the General and Marine Hospital and lobbying for improvements to Collingwood harbour.
– Courtesy: Mary Richardson

design, lift construction and snowmaking. A self-taught engineer, he collaborated with the North American Engineering Company to install Blue Mountain's first modern snowmaking system in 1973. He also invented an improved snowmaking gun. He was placed on the Blue Mountain board of directors by Jozo, who relied on him a great deal. After Jozo's death, Skelton continued to have a strong voice in shaping the long-term growth of the company.

While Jozo's finances had been greatly improved by the success of Blue Mountain Pottery, the improvements to the resort in the 1960s were very expensive and were again building up the debt burden. He was concerned that Blue Mountain should remain a strong public area, and even offered to sell the resort to the Ontario government with this objective in mind. Although some interest was expressed by Queen's Park, nothing came of the idea.

In 1964 an additional capital requirement was imposed by the death of Jozo's long-time partner, Senator Campbell. The Campbell family wished to dispose of their shares, and Jozo bought them, increasing his stake in Blue Mountain Resorts to 78 percent and assuming total ownership of Craigleith Development, a real estate company that he had formed with the Senator. Jozo was dismayed by Campbell's death. He had been

Werner Zotter of Collingwood on course during the Peter Campbell Memorial slalom on Spectacular, c. 1965. – Courtesy: Jack MacMurchy

The Blue Mountain Pottery factory and observation studio located opposite the Gateway Plaza. After the Pottery was sold by Jozo in 1967, it continued to be one of Collingwood's major industries. By the 1970s the product was distributed in over 80 countries. Photo c. 1975.
– Courtesy: Collingwood *Enterprise-Bulletin*

grateful for Campbell's support, knowing that the Senator had safer places to invest his money. On Jozo's initiative the Peter Campbell Memorial Race was established in recognition of the Senator's contribution to the development of Blue Mountain. When Jozo died in 1971 the Campbell family, generous as always, insisted that his name be added, and the event became the Campbell-Weider Memorial.

In order to strengthen his financial position and concentrate on resort development, in 1967 Jozo sold Blue Mountain Pottery for $800,000 to International Silver, a branch of an American-owned conglomerate. From this point the pottery went through a series of owners but continued to be one of Collingwood's leading industries until 1987, when it fell on hard times. After a few months in limbo it was purchased and revived by former manager Bob Blair. Today the glazing process is essentially the same as that employed in the days of Jozo, and some of the original designs are still in production as well.

After he sold the pottery, Jozo retained 10 acres of land across from the pottery factory on the western edge of Collingwood and built a large restaurant, the Gateway, and a little shopping centre in a European style. It featured a planetarium which Jozo intended to develop into a tourist attraction. He was planning to add a 100-room Sheraton hotel and make this complex into a gateway to Blue Mountain, linking the town and the mountain.

The Town and the Mountain

In establishing his Gateway complex Jozo intended to solidify the relationship between Blue Mountain and the town of Collingwood. While the links were always strong, they were sometimes strained. In the 1940s, when the ski operation was getting established, the town was oriented toward industry and agriculture rather than tourism. Its pride was the shipyard and the local hockey team, the Collingwood Shipbuilders. Many of the townspeople and merchants resented the outsiders who tramped into restaurants and stores in ski suits and heavy boots. "We definitely had the feeling that we were not wanted when we tried to book into the Arlington for the weekend," remembers Ted Harrison, who has been skiing at Blue Mountain with his wife, Gertrude, since 1947. "We quickly learned that the best thing to do was to arrive dressed in business clothes; if we had ski jackets on we might be told that all the rooms were taken."

There was still hostility 15 years later when Collingwood was being referred to as the "Ski Capital of Ontario." "Skiers are people, just like you – just like me – just like your son and mine," pleaded an editorial in the Collingwood *Enterprise-Bulletin* in 1963. "They have feelings too and when approached in a belligerent fashion quite naturally react in a like manner. Be understanding. Don't anticipate a hard time from skiers and difficulties might not appear. Collingwood needs the ski trade. You might not think so, but if you didn't have it, you would certainly notice the absence. All this situation needs is a little 'give and take.' There are faults on both sides." The editorial went on to lecture skiers not to expect

Main street of Collingwood in the heyday of shipbuilding, c. 1966. Although the town's main interest was the shipyard, it was already being hailed as the ski capital of Ontario and celebrated that role as well.
– Courtesy: Jack MacMurchy, Credit: Lee Stephenson

Nancy Greene accepting trophy from Mayor Alick H. McDonald of Collingwood for her win in the slalom event of the Peter Campbell Memorial Competition, February 1966.
– Courtesy: Jack MacMurchy, Credit: Fritz Schuller

At left. *Members of the Collingwood Collegiate Ski Team in front of their school, 1947. Left to right: Marcella Plater, Kathleen Robinson, Marie Robinson, Shirley Brophy.*
– Courtesy: Marcella Plater Keith

The Collingwood Chamber of Commerce and local volunteers were active in organizing winter carnivals and special events to promote winter fun. Rob Hisey (left) and Ed Christie (right) pose with their snow sculpture entry, 1978.
– Courtesy: Collingwood Museum, Credit: *Collingwood Times* Archive

Below: *Mrs. D. A. Harvie, a founding director of the Blue Mountain Ski Club, registers Ian and Stuart McKay for the Ontario Junior Championships, held at Blue Mountain in 1951. The boys were the sons of Dr. Donald McKay, who was much esteemed in Collingwood for his medical and community work. At the typewriter is Marg Gooch, representing the Canadian Amateur Ski Association. Marg's husband, Bob Gooch, served as President of the Toronto Ski Club between 1963 and 1966, was active in the CASA, and put in hundreds of hours organizing Alpine and Nordic competitions throughout Ontario.*
– Courtesy: Jack MacMurchy, Credit: Jack Saunders

Greta McGillivray and Helen Weider were inducted into the Collingwood Sports Hall of Fame as a result of their skiing victories in the 1950s. Here they are shown after an Ontario Senior Ladies Tournament, c. 1955. Left to right: Jean Firth, Helen Weider, Greta McGillivray and Joan Goad.
– Courtesy: Jack MacMurchy

Jozo and daughter Katherine pose with local skiers, 1959. Left to right: Jozo Weider, Dave Christie, Katherine Weider, John Blakely and Fritz Schuller. A life-long resident of Collingwood, David Christie won the Ontario Senior "C" Alpine Combined in 1954 and other titles. He was also an active director of the Collingwood Ski Club. John Blakely competed in high school and Ontario meets. Fritz Schuller was a racer and a director of the Collingwood Ski Club. He went on to establish Schuller's Fotography and amassed a collection of fine ski photos over the years. – Courtesy: Jack MacMurchy

to buy a cup of coffee and enjoy unlimited tenancy of their stool or booth. Skiers were also advised not to annoy waitresses, be overly loud and boisterous, or attempt to cheat on restaurant checks, carry glasses of beverages from licensed premises to restaurants, and above all not be abusive.

While as recently as the 1980s, members of the Toronto media have made a sport of eliciting quotes from Collingwooders disgruntled over the influx of skiers and tourists, the townspeople have had greater sympathy for and involvement with the sport than generally acknowledged. It should be remembered that the first facilities on Blue Mountain were established by the Blue Mountain Ski Club, led by prominent town businessmen John Smart and Norman Boadway. Boadway and Smart were successful in getting the town council solidly behind their efforts, and the local media was helpful as well. As early as 1939 the *Enterprise-Bulletin* was proclaiming Collingwood a "Ski Town" and urging citizens to participate in the promotion and development of ski facilities.

When Jozo Weider took over the direction of Blue Mountain from the Blue Mountain and Toronto ski clubs, he was supported through his difficulties by John Smart, Jack Saunders, Herb Chapman and other Collingwood businessmen. Furniture store owner Clare Trott remembers that Jozo was frequently unable to pay his bills and often remunerated Trott and his fellow merchants with Blue Mountain shares. Trott became a life-long confidant of Jozo and his family and served on the Blue Mountain board of directors for 20 years.

The end of an era occurred when the last ship was launched in Collingwood harbour on December 5, 1985, and the yard was closed the following September. The Trott furniture company had been partially dependent on supplying furniture for ships, and in 1989 it ceased operation after 127 years and four generations of Trott ownership. As the traditional Collingwood industries declined, condominium and resort construction took up the slack. Tourism was now clearly the focus for Collingwood and other communities in the Georgian Triangle, and the

Anna and Katherine Weider at the Canadian Junior Championships, 1960. Twin daughters, they were born in Collingwood while the family was living in a cabin next to Blue Mountain Lodge, and they started skiing at the age of four. Anna won the Canadian Junior Downhill in 1960, and the Canadian Junior Slalom the following year. Katherine won numerous junior and senior Ontario titles in the course of her racing career, and achieved major wins in Quebec and France while attending McGill and Grenoble universities. Both girls were proficient in cross-country, as well as in the Alpine events.
– Courtesy: Jack MacMurchy, Credit: B & I Photography

Collingwood Ski Club's 1969 Club Champions. Left to right, rear: Kathy Titus, Katie Payne, John MacMurchy, Peter Wilde, Michael Jaroch. Left to right, front: Tanya Titus, Michelle Jaroch, Sherry Titus, Jill Abbotts. Front: Patricia Christie.
– Courtesy: Jack MacMurchy, Credit: Lee Stephenson

The National Ski Academy, class of 1988-89. Left to right, rear: Mario Blanchet, Alan Adams, Ryan Phillips, Andrea Canning, Steve Bourbonnais, Martha Lee, Gareth Corrigan, Michelle Dehne, Peter Lee, Malcolm Verth, Christy Thorburn, Bill Kritsch, Kelly Jackson, Greg McGreery, Lisa Warll, Graeme Buckrell, Graydon Oldfield, Rob McKendry, Matthew Vermilyea. Left to right, front: Rob Thorburn, Dallas Philp, Jeff Crompton, Jasper Blake, Laura Lassila, Marnie Gibson. – Courtesy: National Ski Academy

A colourful and gregarious businessman, John Will was a popular figure around Blue Mountain and the private clubs. His enormously successful Squire John's Ski Shop on Highway 26 at Craigleith was founded in 1969. It flourished as a result of the fine customer service, painstaking attention to detail, and John's personal warmth. Since John's tragic death in 1986, the business has been carried on by his partner, Helen Kimble. – Courtesy: Helen Kimble

support of the ski pioneers by the Collingwood people proved to have been farsighted.

Over the five decades, Collingwood and the community of permanent residents at Craigleith fielded strong competitors in Ontario and Canadian championships. Most of them belonged to the Blue Mountain Ski Club, which in 1961 was reconstituted as the Collingwood Ski Club. From the start the club was active in organizing competitions and encouraging local racers. It acquired a permanent headquarters in 1961, when a clubhouse was built at the north end of the resort under the direction of club president Jim Russell. Collingwood Collegiate was always a power in Ontario high-school competition, winning provincial championships in 1949, 1972 and 1990. In 1988 an important ski-oriented educational institution was founded in Collingwood: the National Ski Academy, a boarding school for high-school-age students intent on developing their racing skills.

While Collingwood was especially proud of its hockey heroes, it also paid tribute to a number of outstanding local skiers by including them in its Sports Hall of Fame. On the honour roll were four skiers who had anchored the first generation of competitors in the 1940s: Marie and Kathy Robinson, John Keith and Marcella Plater. The 1950s produced Greta McGillivray and Helen Weider. Also inducted were Jozo's twin daughters, Anna and Katherine Weider, who had followed their older sister in becoming Ontario and Canadian junior champions. The twins had a particularly successful season in 1960, when they swept Ontario meets and then led the Ontario team to victory in the Canadian Junior Championships at Thetford Mines, Quebec. Anna won the downhill, while Katherine won a bronze medal in slalom. While attending McGill University in 1964, Katherine added another provincial title to her string of victories, this time the Quebec Senior Alpine Championship.

Another outstanding skier and hall-of-famer from the Sixties was Werner Zotter. He had received a head start in Austria before coming to Collingwood with his parents at the age of nine. An excellent athlete, he quickly adapted to his new surroundings and became proficient in hockey as a goal-keeper. His real talent, however, was demonstrated on ski hills and ski jumps. In 1966 in a feat reminiscent of the Georgas brothers in the 1950s, Zotter captured the Ontario Four-Way Championship, as well as the Canadian Junior Alpine. That same year he won the much-touted Wilkinson Sword speed trials at Georgian Peaks, averaging 84 miles an hour in three runs. Also included in the Collingwood Sports Hall of Fame were the builders and ski pioneers John Smart, Norman Boadway and Jozo Weider.

This print appeared in Bob Kemp's book entitled Places & Faces. Artist's caption: "1972: This is the view from our front windows, looking west. The rich colour scheme created by the sun on a February morning as it rises behind us is lost in a black and white reproduction. The whole effect resembles a large ice cream sherbert." – Courtesy: Barb Kemp, Credit: Bob Kemp

The Township and the Chalets

While Collingwood was the main service centre for Jozo's ski and tourist operation, it was Collingwood Township which held jurisdiction over most matters directly affecting the resort. In the early days, when Jozo was struggling to develop the business, the township was almost entirely an agricultural community. In the 1940s there were cottages along Georgian Bay, but most of them were used only for summer vacations. During the 1950s and 1960s, however, clusters of chalets were built along the bottom edge of the ski area. The nucleus of the first community became the Artist's Studio, built by Robert Kemp. Educated at St. Andrew's College and the Banff School of Fine Arts, Kemp was working as a commercial artist in Toronto when he became increasingly attracted by the beauty of the Blue Mountain area and its recreational opportunities. He built the original studio and residence in 1958, initially calling it the "Wedel Inn," after the ski technique that was popular in the Fifties.

The Artist's Studio was surrounded by tiny chalets of varying styles. The most bizarre was the "Starting Gate." It was originally the starting tower of the Thorncliffe race-track, from where it was trucked to its new location. The neighbouring chalets – Green Door, Green Roof, Debaucherie Inn, Pook, Donkey, Annex, R.C.'s and D (Roman Catholics and Druids) – were hurriedly slapped together by the owners and their friends on weekends. "They were all built with second-hand lumber or logs," remembers Al Butler. The Annex was built out of discarded hydro poles that Butler and his friends bought for $1 each, and Jozo delivered them for $25. They argued among themselves how to split Jozo's bill.

Douglas Carruthers, now a justice of the Ontario Supreme Court, never forgot the hilarious days that he and his friends enjoyed in the shacks around the Artist's Studio near the end of the 1950s. Some of them rented a decrepit cabin called "Sleeply Mila" from Jozo. There was no indoor plumbing, and each weekend they would pick up a drum full of water from the Ski Barn. After an especially cold night someone would have to crawl out of his sleeping bag and use a hammer to break up the thick layer of ice that had formed on top of their buckets. Sometimes they did not go to bed at all. The adjoining cabin was rented by Senator David Walker, a friend of Jozo's who enjoyed getting an early start on his ski

Sunning between the Annex and the Donkey, 1956. Left to right: Hugh Marshall, Don Morgan, Al Butler and Frank Shawpburger.
– Courtesy: Barb Kemp, Credit: Bob Kemp

Portrait in ballpoint pen of Cyril Musil by Robert Kemp, 1975. Describing his neighbour in his book Country Charms, *Kemp wrote: "Cyril Musil has left an indelible mark on this area. He arrived from Europe in the early fifties with nothing but his strong arms and his tenacity . . . The trails he has cut out of this mountainside are too numerous to count."*
– Courtesy: Barb Kemp, Credit: Bob Kemp

vacations. "At eight o'clock in the morning," remembers Carruthers, "Walker was setting out for his day on the mountain, while the fellows would be coming home from a party. He did not approve."

A ramshackle compound of dwellings was constructed by the Czechoslovak immigrant Cyril Musil, who supplemented his ski shop business by renting rooms to skiers. In a portrait of his neighbour, Robert Kemp captured the rugged and weather-beaten features of the ski shop owner. A former international cross-country ski champion, Cyril prided himself on his toughness and endurance. He had fought both the Nazis and Communists before making his home in Canada, having escaped from a Communist prison camp in the dead of winter and struggled through deep snow to the Austrian border with rags and pieces of blankets wrapped around his feet. Claiming that, as a result of this ordeal, he had no feeling in his feet to cause pain, he walked around barefoot even while cutting trails and hauling logs off the mountain.

The chalets were the scene of parties, songfests and pranks. Kemp entertained on the ukulele and drew laughter with his exact imitation of Jozo's Eastern European accent. An account of a New Year's Eve party at the Green Roof mentioned that when the guests went out on the verandah to watch a fireworks display they found that there were too many of them to fit back in again. Some of the events organized by the inhabitants of "shacktown," as Kemp called it, became annual rituals, such as the "Lively Cup," a race on the "V" hill among teams from each cabin; and the "Horse's Ass," a costume race that celebrated its final year, the 25th, in 1990.

In contrast to the haphazard chalet construction near the north end of the resort in the Fifties, the lands at the foot of the mountain to the south underwent a more carefully planned development. In 1956 Jozo persuaded Senator Campbell to form Craigleith Development Limited for the purpose of subdividing part of the flat lands on the Kinsey, Plater and Carmichael farms. The role of land development was as much to build up permanent customers for the ski operation as to make a profit on sales.

Subdivisions were developed along Lucille Wheeler Crescent and Ann Heggtveit Drive, named after the two world champions of the Fifties. Initial prices in 1962 were as low as $750 for a half-acre lot, and Jozo had to literally beg skiers to buy properties at these bargain-basement prices.

Karl Zotter, c. 1967. Zotter's Ski Shop was located at the edge of the chalet community in the Fifties. Karl Zotter came to Blue Mountain from Austria in 1953 and managed Jozo's ski shop before opening his own at the north end.
– Courtesy: Jack MacMurchy, Credit: Fritz Schuller

The mountain and bottom lands from the L-Hill to the "V" Hill, c. 1952. The scattered chalets located at the bottom of the north end were a sign of the development to follow.
– Courtesy: Jack MacMurchy, Credit: Herb Hall

Women skiers at the bottom of the Granny, 1950. Left to right: Ruth Consaul, Bev Baker, Dil Elliott and Bunny Jarvis. Bunny McKendrick, née Jarvis, remembers that they stayed in an uninsulated cabin whose main use was to provide shelter for migrant apple pickers in the fall. "There was a Quebec heater, into which we shoved pieces of coal, newspapers, or anything that was around to keep us warm. I chose my boyfriends on how well they could bank a fire." The walls were lined with works of the owner, an untalented art teacher. "The paintings were ghastly. We got so sick of looking at those tired old tiger lilies that we decided to turn the paintings around. But to our horror, they were painted on the back as well." Conditions improved when she married and moved into "Fort McKendrick," built by her husband, Bruce, in 1953. "We've been remodelling it ever since," she ironically notes.
– Courtesy: Bunny McKendrick

Those who took up his offer and held on to their properties have achieved a gain of nearly 100 times their original investment.

Jozo's creativeness and versatility were very much in evidence in his real estate projects. He did much of his own design work in laying out the land parcels and the access roads, turning his sketches over to an engineer for final-draft plans and surveys. Architectural controls were imposed to ensure reasonable standards for buildings. The quality of his developments was further improved in new subdivisions launched in the later 1960s. The new chalets were served by a water system designed by Jozo's engineers and built by Jozo and his construction manager, Glyn Griffiths. It utilized holding tanks tapped into a stream that flowed down the

Early cabins were small but cosy. – Courtesy: George Czerny

mountain. Land development was surging ahead at an accelerated rate by the time of Jozo's death in 1971, and Jozo's real estate programs were continued throughout the Seventies by the Blue Mountain group of companies.

As at the north end, the community that was formed in the subdivisions at the south end developed its own peculiar folklore and cast of characters. The first chalet lit up on a Friday night would serve as a beacon for the rest of the inhabitants; it was not a location for those bent on maintaining a private life. Twenty years after the rise of the "shacktown"

Après-ski at Art and Pat Yates' cabin, 1948. – Courtesy: Art and Pat Yates

Skiers pose at the Yates' chalet, 1948. Left to right: Jack Weekes, unknown, Doris Weekes, Pat Yates, Art Yates, Ede Williams, Ross Wilson and Wearie Williams. – Courtesy: Art & Pat Yates

Lot sales in the Anne Heggtveit Subdivision began in 1962. Construction in this subdivision at the foot of the Apple Bowl has been completed, c. 1974.
– Courtesy: Blue Mountain Resorts Limited

Residents of the subdivision located at Blue Mountain's south end. Left to right: Jim Bain, Bob Lorne and Ted Henerofsky, c. 1964.
– Courtesy: Bob Lorne

community, the chalet owners still knew how to enjoy life, and their chalets were much more comfortable. The core group of the 1970s was serious about both their skiing and partying. An inseparable fraternity was made up of Bob Lorne, Ted Henerofsky, John Eversfield, Bruce Jardine, Harry Barker, Jim Bain, Bert Bigiel, Bob Leydon, Alex Ponton and Ian Cunningham. As related by Bob Lorne in recent reminiscences, he and his friends had a set pattern in pursuing pleasures on the hills and in the bars. They started early at the L-Hill, O-Hill, or South Chair and worked their way over to the Toronto Ski Club, where they would "share one very long table and many pitchers of beer." Then there would be a leisurely trip back to the south, perhaps stopping at someone's chalet.

Plunger twirler, "Ms. Flusher '76" (Reg Margesson), at Blue Mountain's Winter Carnival, represents the residents of the Anne Heggtveit Subdivision, who founded an annual "Flushers' Follies" spring spree.
– Courtesy: Collingwood Museum, Credit: *Collingwood Times* Archive

The 50-metre jump built by Jozo in 1970 was not the first ski jump at Blue Mountain. At the south end of the Apple Bowl, Jozo had erected a 25-metre jump in 1954 that had been used for provincial jumping meets and Nordic competitions. The new jump was named in memory of Pete Pettersen, a Norwegian immigrant who had developed strong ski jumping programs in Ontario in the 1950s. Jozo's new jump was the site of the North American Jumping Championships in 1971.
– Courtesy: Blue Mountain Resorts Limited, Credit: Fritz Schuller

A European and a Quebecker stage a two-man protest against Ontario's arcane liquor laws. Egged on by Jozo, Ernie McCulloch illegally drinks beer at the base of Apple Bowl, 1970. Note that both are wearing buckle boots; Jozo's plastic Langes have the vinyl "Langeflow" lining.
– Courtesy: Marijane Thomas, Credit: Fritz Schuller

The activities of Lorne and his buddies at the south end seem quite tame in comparison to some of the shenanigans in nearby Tyrolean Village and the surrounding chalets. It is remembered that a party in that area attracted the attention of the police to such an extent that a small army of OPP officers was mustered at the site, equipped with dogs, tear gas and a paddy wagon. At least 35 officers stealthily approached through the woods and then burst into the chalet in search of marijuana, but only one arrest was made. A visit by the police to the VAT, also at Tyrolean, turned up a bed that had been removed from the Collingwood hospital in an open convertible, an illegal beer-vending machine and stolen highway signs.

The farmers who controlled local government initially were wary of Jozo and the chalet owners whom he attracted to Blue Mountain. They gradually became more accepting as they or their sons began taking jobs on tows and trails, and municipal tax payments began to flow into the township's office in Clarksburg. There was one issue, however, on which Jozo failed to get his way. From the day he arrived to nearly the day he died, Collingwood Township voted "dry" under the local option legislation, which meant that no liquor, wine or beer could be served at Blue Mountain or anywhere else in the township. Hotel operators in the town of Collingwood fared better. As a result of a plebiscite in 1961, the Mountain View and the Tremont were able to open taverns.

Marooned in the "Sahara" of Collingwood Township, Jozo organized campaigns to try to get similar privileges for the resort, but his efforts in the township failed repeatedly, owing to the fierce counterattacks mounted by religious-minded individuals who were already angered by the resort's Sunday operations. "Ski resorts threaten church attendance," a newspaper headline had screamed in 1941. Some churchmen found it outrageous that, after having stolen part of their congregation, the resort operators wanted to serve liquor to it as well. Jozo's campaigns were made all the more difficult by the requirement of a 60-percent majority to make the township "wet." The scrutineer at the poll was a severe-looking woman who was obviously a "dry" sympathizer. "She would look at you with those gimlet eyes," remembers Marijane Thomas, who helped Jozo in one of his unsuccessful pro-liquor campaigns in 1969, "and size you up as a 'wet.' You felt as if you were being condemned to go straight to Hell."

Shortly before his death, Jozo did receive the right to have liquor at the resort, but it could only be served along with meals in a sit-down restaurant. "Rubber sandwiches" were sold at nominal prices to help get around the problem. It was illegal to have a drink on Sundays when standing on one's feet. A resort licence for the base lodge was acquired after Jozo's death, but many cumbersome rules remained in force until the mid-1970s. "You'd have the entire province swimming in booze," Gordon Canning was told when he pleaded the resort's case with James Mackie, the tough ex-police chief who was chairman of the Ontario Liquor Board. Mackie's prophecy almost came true. When a tavern licence was finally granted, Canning had the indoor swimming pool of the Blue Mountain Inn boarded over and replaced by a bar. Appropriately, it was named "Jozo's."

Reeve D.J. McNichol was one of the earliest of the local community leaders to appreciate and support Jozo's efforts. Reeve McNichol's personal history is a story of survival and tenacity both as a farmer-busi-

This contemporary photo (1990) of the bottom lands viewed from the Apple Bowl shows the vast amount of development that has occurred over the last three decades, especially during the 1980s.
– Courtesy: Doug Czerny, Credit: Doug Czerny

nessman and local politician. He was born in his family's farmhouse near Ravenna and has lived there all of his life, carrying on farming and timber-cutting on the escarpment. He supplied cedar poles for Jozo's rope tows in the 1950s, though sometimes it took to the end of the winter before he would be paid. McNichol was first elected to the township council in the fall of 1949. He became reeve in 1955, and except for one brief interruption and rare political defeat, he has held the position for the last 35 years. He was on hand for the opening of Jozo's pomalift in 1955 and was still in office 31 years later, in 1986, when a multi-million-dollar sewage treatment plant was officially opened at the eastern edge of the township. Among his political accomplishments, the one he is most proud of is the unprecedented feat of being elected Warden of Grey County for three terms.

Although Reeve McNichol and Jozo Weider were on opposite sides of the fence in federal and provincial politics – McNichol was a Tory and Jozo was a Grit – the two saw eye to eye as far as the municipality was concerned, and they were in many ways similar in character. Both were tireless in pursuit of their goals and both wanted to see the Blue Mountain area develop into a four-seasons resort community. Neither would back off from a fight if he felt strongly about an issue. As a result of McNichol's continuous badgering of county and provincial politicians, the roads into the resort and the entire road network in the township were vastly improved. He was instrumental in bringing about advanced land-use plans for the Beaver Valley and Craigleith, and in persuading the provincial government at the beginning of the 1980s to finance construction of water and sewage services for the township. The services, whose

Jozo held outdoor parties throughout most of his life at Blue Mountain. Here, he is shown hosting a spring Gluhwein *in 1965.*
– Courtesy: Jack MacMurchy, Credit: Ian MacMurchy

cost amounted to $20 million by 1987, allowed full-scale resort development to go ahead in the township.

After Jozo's death, Reeve McNichol led the way in the foundation of the Jozo Weider Information Centre to recognize Jozo's contribution to the area and promote tourism. The building was constructed on land owned by Blue Mountain Pottery, next to the pottery factory. The operation grew into the Georgian Triangle Tourist Association and Convention Bureau. Managed from its inception by Shiela Metras, the GTTA has played an important role in co-ordinating tourism development not only in Collingwood and Collingwood Township, but among several municipalities within the Georgian Triangle.

Toward the end of his long career at Blue Mountain, Jozo was in command of a ski-and-tourist empire that included a flourishing 800-acre ski resort, a major land development at the foot of Blue Mountain and an outpost in Collingwood at the "gateway" to the ski area. Easing out of the pottery business allowed him to relax a little. He delegated more authority and reduced his work schedule, although it was still twice as heavy as that of most men. He took more time off for travelling, continued to ski, and during the summer would sally out on the waves of Georgian Bay in a kayak, his favourite watercraft. He indulged his love of

Jozo Weider, patriarch of a ski empire, in front of his chalet at the south end of Blue Mountain, March 1971. – Courtesy: Blue Mountain Resorts Limited, Credit: Fritz Schuller

the Nordic sports by building a 50-metre ski jump with a view to hosting international competitions. The landing hill was near the bottom of the Apple Orchard, the southernmost property of the resort which he had purchased in 1970, paying $160,000 for 140 acres, his biggest expenditure ever for a parcel of land. He exercised his customary frugality in constructing the jump, building the girders out of used steel beams purchased from Teperman's. The North American Ski Jumping Championships were held at Blue Mountain in 1971, but the attendance was disappointing and the jump received almost no use after that. Ski jumping had been declining in favour of downhill skiing, and a Nordic program did not materialize at the resort. The jump became a hazard and was torn down after Jozo's death.

After selling the pottery in 1967 Jozo built an imposing chalet between the Apple Orchard and the Big Baby and moved there from the old farmhouse. The chalet was designed by a Czechoslovak architect and had an emblem on the exterior wall depicting a Slovak folk hero, a bandit similar to the English Robin Hood. "I have painted the Czechoslovak Robin Hood on my wall," he told his audience at the annual meeting of the Toronto Ski Club. "Your Robin Hood stole from the rich and gave money to the poor. I steal from the rich and keep it," he joked, informing the skiers that ticket prices were to be increased by one dollar for the coming season. He had grown a beard which gave him a patriarchal appearance, and he continued to be a genial host to the patrons of the resort, despite the fact that there were now so many of them. In 1968, when his daughter Katherine married Gordon Canning, he staged a celebration on the mountain, to which all skiers were invited. Toward the end of his life he was still holding "sugaring off" parties outside the log snack bar at the South Chair, doling out hot mulled wine or maple syrup from a huge iron kettle. This is how many remember him.

Gordon Canning led the way in the expansion of Blue Mountain after Jozo's death in 1971. He replaced George Weider as President in 1978.
– Courtesy: Blue Mountain Resorts Limited, Credit: Dan McCracken

PART V

After Jozo

On October 4, 1971, 30 years after he had founded Blue Mountain Resorts Limited, Jozo was killed in an automobile accident near Shelburne. There was a massive turnout for the memorial service at the resort's Base Lodge. Jozo had known hundreds of skiers by their first names, many of them since the era of the ski trains and the Blue Mountain Lodge in the 1940s. He was liked by his employees for his warmth and his concern for their welfare. He had helped and sheltered immigrants from Czechoslovakia and other lands. He had been generous with advice and assistance to businessmen in the area and had helped several of them set up their own enterprises. He was the largest single donor to the Canadian Ski Association, and encouraged and assisted the racing programs that were to produce world-class competitors from Ontario in the 1970s. In 1983 Jozo was posthumously placed on the Honour Roll of Canadian Skiing by the Canadian Ski Museum, which had recently initiated the Honour Roll as a method of recognizing the great men and women of the sport.

Not only was Jozo's death a numbing loss for his family, friends and employees, but it created temporary uncertainty about the company's future. The company passed into an estate, whose beneficiaries were my mother, my three sisters and myself. Our family opted to carry on the resort and continue the improvements that Jozo had begun. I and my brothers-in-law Gordon Canning and Don McGillivray became the key decision-makers. We were assisted by outside directors, especially John Hethrington from the Benson and Hedges Tobacco Company, and later Urban Joseph, a vice-president of the Toronto Dominion Bank. With new depth on the board, the company continued the expansion program that Jozo had launched in the Sixties and pursued it even more aggressively.

New Leaders, New Projects and a New Image

Gordon Canning emerged as a natural leader. He directed the expansion program that solidified Blue Mountain's predominance as Ontario's leading ski resort and made it into a premier summer resort as well. Gordon was relatively new to the ski operation. He had been a systems programmer at Imperial Oil before apprenticing under Jozo and being given a management position at Blue Mountain in 1970, five months before Jozo's death. As Gordon was a quick study, his lack of experience was not an insurmountable handicap, and in many ways he was ideally suited to manage a major business. He had graduated from Queen's University as a mathematics major, obtained an MA at Waterloo, and an MBA from York. His facility with numbers and logical approach as a result of his computer training helped him analyze opportunities rapidly and set out priorities from among the range of alternatives that faced the company. Whereas Jozo had made many decisions by instinct and impulse, then insisted that they be carried out, Gordon was more systematic in studying new projects and in building consensus among managers and directors before launching new undertakings. The new style was more suited for a business that had evolved from the entrepreneurial to the corporate phase of development. Most of the decisions were profitable, and, what was equally important, Gordon developed a strong management group and well-trained staff. In an industry where employee turnover was notoriously high, the majority of Blue Mountain's employees put in long terms of service – in some cases a lifetime – with the company.

The demands for improvements continued to be pressing. The rapid growth of the skier market in the Sixties continued into the first half of the Seventies. Ontario ski areas had 2.4 million skier visits in the 1970-71 season. By 1975-76 the number had climbed to almost 4 million. The winter visitors were leaving their dollars not just at the resort but all over the area. A survey of Collingwood retail establishments indicated that in 1977-78 skiers contributed $7.1 million to the local retail service sector. From studies that were done of Blue Mountain's skiers (the major market had always been Toronto and the heavily populated suburban corridor between Toronto and Burlington) it was recognized that they were becoming increasingly affluent, sophisticated and demanding, reflecting the general North American profile. Almost two-thirds of those who had purchased the new Head skis at the end of the 1960s, at $115 to $150 a pair, were college-educated. The days when skiers were content to cram themselves into bunk beds in unheated shacks and ride the rope tow all day were over. The younger generation wanted not only chairlifts, but chairlifts with padded seats. Providing entertainment at the bottom of the hill was as important as moving skiers on the lifts. Many came to resorts not

Mother Nature has taken a break, c. 1974
– Courtesy: Blue Mountain Resorts Limited

Blue Mountain's Area Manager Bill Skelton adjusts a snow gun, 1973.
– Courtesy: Blue Mountain Resorts Limited

just to ski but also to meet members of the opposite sex. When a reporter interviewed a woman at Squaw Valley in 1965 and asked her why she skied, he got quite a response: " 'Men, M-E-N. They're here in bunches, and so am I, baby,' answers slinky, sloe-eyed Betty Reames as she selects a couch strategically placed midway between the fireplace and the bar."

With these requirements in mind, the company continued Jozo's modernization efforts, improving its cafeterias and facilities for après-ski entertainment. Jozo's Bar was opened and the liquor began to flow. It was hard to get into the place unless one developed a relationship with the doorkeeper. One of the regulars spent $7,800 in bar bills over one season. Another expensive tradition practised by a few customers was the occasional purchase of a round of drinks for the whole bar. Two patrons flipped a coin one evening to determine who would do the honours, and the one who lost spent $750 on B-52s and other expensive liqueurs.

Uphill transportation was not neglected. Three new chairlifts were built between 1971 and 1980: the triple chairs at the Inn, L-Hill and Big Baby. New base lodges were built at the Inn Triple Chair and at the south. The investment in lifts during this period was more than $1 million. Another $1.5 million was spent on the base lodges and bars. The

Blue Mountain's Hill Hostess Mavis Quigley assists skiers, c. 1974. In the background is one of Blue Mountain's innovative "Get Moving" boards. Looking on are Doug and Andrew Hethrington, whose father conceived the information boards.
– Courtesy: Blue Mountain Resorts Limited

investments were financed by means of loans from the Bank of Commerce and the Ontario Development Corporation, assisted by profits that were immediately ploughed back into the operation.

In 1976 the contract with Ernie McCulloch expired, and Blue Mountain took over the ski shop and rental operation that had been in McCulloch's hands. The retail and rental services were expanded. The ski shop was taken over by my sister Katherine Canning. In doing so she was following in the footsteps of our mother, who had managed the ski shop in the old sheep barn in the 1950s.

The face of Blue Mountain was significantly developed and reshaped at the southern part of the resort. The South Base Lodge was built near the southern entrance. The triple chair at the Big Baby provided efficient access to the gently rolling, wide-open slope and made it ideal for beginners. The installation of a chair there allowed the doubling of the run's length; it had previously been accessed from shorter lifts, a pomalift and T-bar. In 1979 the Big Baby and the adjoining O-Hill were opened for night skiing after an extensive lighting system was installed. The Big Baby had been the south L-Hill in the original LOL pattern that Ross Larway had remarked on when he made his approach from Stayner in 1935. Forty-four years later, the Big Baby and the neighbouring slope to the north, a developed version of the old O-Hill, could be spotted from the same point, now ablaze with lights. The entire three-kilometre stretch between the Big Baby and the North Chair was a continuous pattern of trails and slopes, serviced by seven chairlifts and six surface lifts. Revenues passed the $1 million mark in 1971, and weekend crowds were as large as 5,000 by 1975.

While these improvements were vitally necessary, there was another move made by the company that was even more important. Immediately after Jozo's death, the decision was made to implement a project that Jozo had been studying, the installation of a snowmaking system to cover most of the resort's slopes. In the post-Jozo era snowmaking became the resort's lifeblood. By virtually guaranteeing continuous skiing throughout the 100-day season, the production of man-made snow justified the construction of expensive lift, hill-grooming and base lodge facilities.

A racer takes a jump during the 1974 Pro Race.

– Courtesy: Blue Mountain Resorts Limited

A modern building for the new era. Carpentry crew directed by Glyn Griffiths in front of the new base lodge, the Inn Café, 1976. The cafeteria, with its intricate beam work, was designed by Toronto architect Paul Hughes, who was also a ski instructor and active in the Toronto Ski Club. Left to right: Karl Gerschwiler, George Chaudet, Mike Amstadt, Glyn Griffiths, Keith Dooks. The men are wearing the uniform jackets that had been recently introduced.
– Courtesy: Blue Mountain Resorts Limited

In 1972, in accordance with plans that Jozo had been making for a larger system, the company borrowed $500,000 from the Bank of Commerce and installed underground pipes, water pumps and a bank of air compressors, allowing coverage of 60 percent of the area. Snowmaking helped the company survive the mild winter of 1972-73 and even show a slight profit. There were 120 acres under snowmaking by 1975. The improved snow conditions supported the heavier traffic on the hills and made Blue Mountain a safer bet as a winter holiday destination for families in Ontario and as far away as Michigan, Ohio, New York and Illinois.

In the years immediately following Jozo's death, many ideas flowed from the fertile mind of John Hethrington, a marketing executive with the Benson and Hedges Tobacco Company. Hethrington, who had raced at Blue Mountain during the 1950s, joined the Blue Mountain board in 1972. Under Hethrington's direction, the resort tidied its signs, adopted a smart new logo, hoisted a new slogan ("Get A Better Run For Your Money") and put the staff into attractive uniforms. Systematic customer surveys and interviews were introduced, and it was found, to no one's surprise, that line-ups were the number-one complaint. To help solve the problem Hethrington suggested the use of electronic signs, the "Get Moving" boards, which announced the waiting times at each lift at the resort, allowing a skier to head for the lift that had the shortest line. The boards were installed at each lift and base lodge and worked well, becoming a permanent feature of the resort.

Former Olympic triple gold medallist Jean Claude Killy takes time out during the Benson & Hedges 100's Grand Prix, 1973.
– Courtesy: Blue Mountain Resorts Limited, Credit: Fritz Schuller

The popular Spider Sabich receives congratulations from John Hethrington of Benson & Hedges.
– Courtesy: Blue Mountain Resorts Limited, Credit: Fritz Schuller

In 1973, in association with John Hethrington and Benson and Hedges, Blue Mountain hosted its first international professional dual slalom tournament. Promoters based in the United States had organized a Grand Prix circuit featuring the world's finest slalom racers. The competitions were spectacular and attracted national television coverage. The skiers on the Pro Tour stormed through gates interspersed with five-foot jumps, in search of $400,000 in prize money in the 14 races on the circuit. Sometimes there were violent collisions when racers veered onto the neighbouring course after losing their balance on certain jumps. In one such crash, the two head-to-head racers wiped out, taking with them a race official and a TV cameraman in an impossible tangle of bodies and equipment.

When the Grand Prix Pro Tour arrived at Blue Mountain the hottest performer on the circuit was Vladimir "Spider" Sabich, a zestful Californian who not only skied fast but also enjoyed motorcycle racing, piloting airplanes and escorting glamorous women. At a post-race party in the Base Lodge most male eyes were fixed on Claudine Longet, the ravishingly beautiful movie actress who accompanied him. Three years later she brought Sabich's adventurous life to an abrupt end by accidentally shooting him with his own gun in his home in Aspen. There were no witnesses to the shooting, and it was later determined that the safety catch of the death instrument, a .22 calibre pistol, was defective. After a sensational trial, with the evidence being hotly contested between the district attorney and the defence counsel, Longet was convicted of criminally negligent homicide and sentenced to 30 days in the Pitkin County Jail.

The organizers of the Pro Tour had hoped to make the dual slalom tournament an annual event, like other big-name sports tournaments, but it was a complex affair to organize and did not produce enough revenues from spectator fees and television royalties to justify the expense. In February 1979 the event was run at Blue Mountain for the last time, in this instance as part of the Labatt Pro Challenge. While the effort required in mounting the Pro Tour had been enormous, it had been worthwhile. The dual slaloms, the "Get Moving" boards, Jozo's, and the massive investments in new lifts and lodges had definitely added some sizzle to the Seventies.

Ski Patrollers Shirley Rhodes and Linda Fitzgerald at the base of the North Poma, c. 1962. – Courtesy: Charles Garrad

Dr. Doug Firth and Katie Wallace at Blue Mountain, 1968.
– Courtesy: Blue Mountain Resorts Limited

Fred Scambatti presents the Carling Cup to the winning Ski Patrol team. Left to right: Fred Scambatti, Egon Holzwarth, Peter Bowman, Brian Glaysher, Richard Lee and Gar Maywood, 1961.
– Courtesy: Brian & Shirley Glaysher, Credit: Lee Stephenson

The Ski Patrol and the Ski School

While huge changes occurred at Blue Mountain during the 1970s and 1980s, there were a number of traditions that provided continuity and that had contributed to the congenial atmosphere since the earliest days. Of all the institutions at the mountain, the Ski Patrol and the Ski School are the oldest and most important.

On January 27, 1990, members of the Central Zone of the Canadian Ski Patrol turned out in force on Blue Mountain to form an honour guard for the man who had founded the patrol in Canada, Dr. Douglas Firth. At the beginning of the 1940s he had begun training patrollers in the St. John Ambulance system and giving them supplementary courses in the treatment of winter injuries. In 1941 The Canadian Ski Patrol System was established as an institution under the auspices of the Canadian Amateur Ski Association (CASA) and with Dr. Firth as chairman.

By 1942 there were already 40 trained patrollers in the Toronto Ski Club, and the patrol was issuing safety instructions to club members. The recommended rules of behaviour sound somewhat fatuous and impractical by today's standards, when there are so many skiers on the hill. In a message in *The Ski-Runner* in 1942 the patrol advised beginning skiers to "be ready for anything" and to imagine that a skier, a dog or, incredibly, a tree could suddenly pop up ahead. They were to heed warning flags and signs, confine attention solely to their own skiing, and refrain from looking around or waving to fellow skiers. It was mandatory to shout "TRACK" when they came up behind a skier to pass him. "Don't whisper this, as the request isn't necessarily confidential." If a skier saw an obstacle on the hill, he was expected to remove it, and the patrol warned against building jumps in the middle of a trail. Those climbing were to do so at the side of the hill, and anyone who made a sitzmark was expected to fill it in and pack it smooth. Skiers were also advised to avoid accidents on the train or around the clubhouse by carrying their equipment in the approved manner, with the hoops of the poles held close to the armpits and the handles extended behind the shoulder.

The little organization founded by Firth has grown into a major national service institution. It had a budget of $11 million in 1981, with an elaborate system of zones and districts in place throughout Canada. Although its training and organization have become increasingly sophisticated over the years, the patrollers continue to be volunteers motivated by love of the sport and concern for their fellow skiers. They still do much of their own fund-raising, especially through the sale of their patrol buttons. Since the volunteers were available primarily on weekends, Blue Mountain began employing one professional patroller in 1969. By 1989 there were 12 full-timers. An additional 65 volunteer patrollers are now on the mountain during busy weekend days. Dr. Firth is 78 years old and has been patrolling at the resort every winter since he founded the patrol in

The site of the Blue Mountain Ski School at the north end of Blue Mountain, c. 1945. – Courtesy: Collingwood Museum

In recognition of his long service in developing the Canadian Ski Patrol System, George Weider congratulates Dr. Doug Firth during the official opening of the Dr. Doug trail, January 1990.
– Courtesy: Blue Mountain Resorts Limited, Credit: Dan McCracken

1941. In 1990, when a new trail was opened underneath the South Chair, it was named Dr. Doug in his honour.

The instructional tradition is also a vital part of the Blue Mountain story. Early ski instruction at the resort was carried out under regulations provided by the Canadian Amateur Ski Association. Instructors' badges were issued to candidates who passed tests in one of the three categories: gold, silver or bronze. In 1942 the mandatory tests were fairly elaborate and included techniques for hill-climbing (herringboning, sidestepping and kickturning), as well as downhill manoeuvres. Candidates were tested for correct form in the "downhill lunging position," right and left stem christiannas and stop jump turns in soft snow. Aspirants for silver and gold badges were required to negotiate a slalom course that included flushes and hairpin turns.

Herb Hall (second from right), wearing the BMR insignia, and Clint Melville (far right), Technical Director of the Canadian Ski Alliance, with Quebec instructors, 1946.
– Courtesy: Jack MacMurchy

Many of the lessons in the 1940s were taught by Jozo, who had acquired his instructor's badge while teaching at Quebec resorts. Also early on the scene was Herb Hall, who taught at Blue Mountain and later at the new private club at Osler. Hall, who has lived in Collingwood since 1945, when he came here after war service overseas, is a colourful raconteur and survivor of the era of the Blue Mountain Lodge, where he instructed for Jozo in the 1946-47 ski season. He was well qualified, having gone through the ladder of the CASA program and earned, along with colleague Clint Melville, the maple leaf of an RSI (Registered Ski Instructor) with the Canadian Ski School Alliance. The Alliance was based

A Canadian Ski Instructors' Alliance class being examined by Elton Irwin at the left. The group from left to right: Harry Brown, Matt Kloos, Bill Pinkerton, Dave Gaudin, Shiela Soulsby, Gloria Clements, Mike Jaroch, Bob Hearn, Jim Georgas, Paul Mathews, Fred Newton and Bernie Cryderman, January 1960. – Courtesy: Jack MacMurchy, Credit: Herb Hall

Blue Mountain's 1962-1963 Ski School. Left to right, rear: Paul Mathews, Don Barnes, Dave Hoar, Glyn Griffiths, Bob Morgan, Bob Lorne, Mike Jaroch. Left to right, front: Helen Hayduk, Lorne "Oakie" O'Connor (Director) and Libby Grant. – Courtesy: Mike & Mary Jaroch

Blue Mountain's 1964-1965 Ski School. Left to right, rear: Don Barnes, Scotty Bain, Werner Zotter, Ken Inglis, Mike Jaroch, Bernie Cryderman, Bob Kerschbaumer, Bob Lorne. Left to right, front: Sue Waters, Paul Mathews, Lorne "Oakie" O'Connor (Director), Helen O'Connor and Ron McCarl. – Courtesy: Mike & Mary Jaroch, Credit: Fritz Schuller

in Quebec, and Hall thinks that he and Melville were the first Ontarians to obtain the maple leaf badge. The prevailing technique was the rotation method, which was illustrated by telling pupils to "Hug a Fat Man" or "Drive a Buick," the hands being extended at about the same length as the wide steering wheels in Buicks at the time.

In addition to ski instruction, Hall's duties included first aid and other tasks on the hill. At the end of each day of skiing he had to remove the six-volt batteries from the engines that powered the tows and take them down the hill on a toboggan to be warmed up in the Lodge, so that they would be strong enough for the next morning's operations. In the evening or on days when conditions were poor, he helped Jozo entertain the guests with songfests, skits and magic shows.

John and Ross Anderson (not related) headed the ski school in the early 1950s, when the Ski Barn was in its heyday, and were succeeded by Austrian racer Henri Moser. An outstanding chief instructor in the 1960s was Lorne O'Connor, who won the prestigious Ryan Cup at Mt. Tremblant in 1962. Rudy Hiegelsberger was in charge from 1967 to 1969.

Rudy Hiegelsberger, senior member of the Canadian Ski Instructors' Alliance and Assistant Director of the Ernie McCulloch Ski School at Blue Mountain, forerunning Class "C" Championships held on Spectacular, 1970.
– Courtesy: Jack MacMurchy, Credit: Ian Gillespie

Ernie McCulloch made his first mark on the history of Canadian skiing when he defeated the French team at Mt. Tremblant at age 20, then went on to many more legendary achievements. He was chief instructor at Blue Mountain from 1969 to 1976. – Courtesy: Jack MacMurchy

The years 1970 to 1976 belonged to the legendary Ernie McCulloch, who put his own stamp on the mountain. McCulloch was probably the finest all-around skier in Canadian ski history. He was born in Trois-Rivières, Quebec, and started skiing at the age of four. As a teenager he won meets in cross-country and jumping, and then went on to become a fearless and brilliant downhiller. At the Quebec Kandahar in 1949 he defeated the entire French ski team, an electrifying victory, as North Americans were considered to have virtually no chance against European racers at the time. In 1951-52 he showed that this was no fluke by being the first and only skier to make a "grand slam" of the four major competitions in North America: the National Giant Slalom, the North American Championships, the National Downhill Championships and the Harriman Cup.

Bottoms Up! Pepi Gramshammer (left), 1962 winner of the combined title in the Canadian Professional Ski Championships, and Ernie McCulloch, top Canadian winner, invert their Bell's Scotch Cups in a toast to victory following the ski championships at Georgian Peaks, 1962.
– Courtesy: Jack MacMurchy, Credit: Herb Hall

The 1971-72 Ernie McCulloch Ski School. Left to right, rear: Mike Robbins, Larry McMahon, Barry Day, Albert Gobo, Don Lowes, Hans Gruber, Gary Empey, Terry Bramham, Jurg Gfeller, Bob Kerschbaumer, Hans Tinsi, Barry Wilkinson, Steve [?], Peter Birney, Paul Fujino, Stan Astbury, Gord Layhew, Dutch Mills. Left to right, front: Jan Welsh, Susan Kill, Jean Layhew, Rudy Hiegelsberger (Assistant Director), Fred Chambers (Assistant Director), Mary Fujino, Ernie McCulloch (Director), Ursula Gruber, Pierre Chauvin (Assistant Director), Paul Hughes (Assistant Director), Chris Hughes, Ruth Ontionio. Absent: Mike Jaroch.
– Courtesy: Blue Mountain Resorts Limited, Credit: Fritz Schuller

Equally distinguished was Ernie's record as a coach and teacher. He became a legend as head of the Mt. Tremblant ski school. At various times he coached the U.S. and Canadian Olympic teams and was president and chief examiner of the Canadian Ski Instructors' Alliance. In 1969 he was elected to the U.S. Ski Hall of Fame, an honour usually reserved for Americans and seldom bestowed on someone still active in the sport.

McCulloch was enticed to Blue Mountain by Jozo as part of Jozo's major promotion and expansion program. He quickly developed a highly professional ski school that consisted of 60 instructors. Ernie was known as a demanding taskmaster but not a grim one; he seldom missed a party and could outdrink and outparty instructors half his age. He was short and lithe, with a thin face and whimsical expression, and was quick in both wit and movement. He had a commanding, almost Napoleonic presence and brooked no challenge to his authority.

Ernie enjoyed playing tricks on his pupils and fellow instructors. Some of his practical jokes caused considerable inconvenience to the victims. On a particularly sunny day, his assistant-director, Pierre Chauvin, asked him whether he had any protective lotion. Ernie excused himself and returned with a bowl of icing that he had scraped from a leftover birthday cake. He told Chauvin that it was sun screen and to put it on. At the end of the day, Chauvin turned up with his face burned red as a lobster. Another instructor was encouraged to switch the liners in ski coach Bob Kerschbaumer's boots before Kerschbaumer made his habitual morning run down the mountain from his chalet on top of the escarpment. The entire ski school was aware of the prank and lined up in laughter while Kerschbaumer skied down the Apple Bowl in great discomfort to join them.

Showing the flawless form that earned her a level four instructor's certificate, Lynn Warll takes a bump at Georgian Peaks, 1981.
– Courtesy: Blue Mountain Resorts

Right: *Ron Westlake became Blue Mountain's Ski School Director in 1983.*
– Courtesy: Blue Mountain Resorts Limited

An adult ski group, c. 1975. Left to right: Dawn Askin, Doris Hiegelsberger, Judy Plater, Geordie Couttie, Ted Henerofsky, Alex Ponton, Rusty MacDonald, Hugh Knowles, Carol Leydon, Wayne King, Bob Leydon, Glen Milne, Bert Bigiel and Jim Bain. Absent: Alex Taylor and Bruce Jardine.
– Courtesy: Blue Mountain Resorts Limited

McCulloch was as well schooled in the theory of the sport as he was skilled in the practice of it. He authored two best-selling books and wrote dozens of articles on ski instruction. He had a matchless command of edge control, weight transfer and all the components of ski technique. He was comfortable in any kind of snow conditions and on any kind of equipment. Long-time Blue Mountain skier and former Hamilton Tiger-Cat football player John Metras, who owned a chalet at the foot of the Apple Bowl, recalls watching Ernie doing elegant parallel turns through deep snow and big bumps on Mogul Alley. When Ernie arrived at the bottom, Metras noticed that he was wearing only a pair of narrow cross-country skis without steel edges, and cross-country boots and bindings.

McCulloch was followed by Don Bilodeau, Lynn Warll, and the current incumbent, Ron Westlake. Born in Collingwood, Ron excelled in skiing and led the Collingwood high-school team to an Ontario Federation of Secondary Schools championship in 1972. He also distinguished himself as a racer on the Southern Ontario Zone team. While Ron has won many competitions and has been unbeatable as a pacesetter in Molstar Challenges, his most memorable victory was obtained in the Great Three Pin Race held on the Happy Valley trail in 1979. Under conditions reminiscent of the hairy downhills of the 1930s, the 35 competitors, wearing cross-country skis and bindings, pushed off all together in a LeMan's start and jostled and lurched their way to the finish line beside the Ski Barn.

The Arctic saga of Jeff MacInnis of the Toronto Ski Club proves that the spirit of adventure that marked the skiers of the Forties is still alive today. After competing in World Cup downhills in the 1982-83 season, he turned to a new challenge. In 1986 he and a companion, Mike Beedell, embarked on a 2,300-mile journey through the North West Passage aboard their 18-foot catamaran, Perception. *Sailing through storm winds that could chill them to minus 30 F, and frequently dragging their boat over razor-sharp ice, they had many narrow escapes from death and became the first explorers to negotiate the Passage by wind power alone.*

– Courtesy: Jeff MacInnis, Credit: Mike Beedell

Liisa Savijarvi and Kellie Casey at Nakiska, 1987. – Courtesy: Kellie Casey

Kellie Casey, Badgastein, Austria, 1988. – Courtesy: National Alpine Ski Team

From Apple Bowl to Kitzbuhel

The high quality of ski instruction at Blue Mountain and the Toronto Ski Club helped produce world-class racers during the 1980s. While the subject is a major one that deserves its own book, the feats of some outstanding competitors can be briefly outlined here. Two of these fine competitors were women, and they invite comparison with the first generation of female competitors who waxed their wooden skis in the basement of Blue Mountain Lodge.

Whereas the women of the Forties wore gabardine knickers and fur-trimmed bonnets, the female racing stars of the 1980s donned crash helmets, squirmed into skin-tight lycra suits, and cruised downhill courses at speeds that would have been illegal in an automobile.

Along with Todd Brooker and Liisa Savijarvi, Kellie Casey initially developed her technique on the hills of Blue Mountain and was a protégée of Rudy Hiegelsberger. The daughter of John Casey, a former lineman on the University of Toronto and Toronto Argonaut football teams, Kellie grew up in Craigleith and attended high schools in Meaford and Collingwood. She achieved international recognition by amassing 55 points and first place in the Nor-Am Downhill standings over the 1985 season. These successes earned her the only available new place on the National Team. She added depth to the talented Canadian women's team and achieved numerous strong finishes, including a fifth place on her favourite downhill course at Val d'Isère in 1987. She spent four years in World Cup competition before retiring in 1989, hampered by injuries incurred at the Calgary Olympics the previous year.

Born in Bracebridge, Ontario, Liisa Savijarvi began racing at the age of eight and came up through the Southern Ontario Division program after getting started at the Toronto Ski Club. A versatile skier, she obtained a level two instructor's certificate and was proficient in slalom, giant slalom, downhill and super-G. Enjoying an excellent season in 1979, she was named to the National Alpine Training Squad and had her first taste of international competition in a World Cup race at Mont Ste. Anne in March 1980. She graduated to the National Alpine Team in 1985 and achieved sensational results on the World Cup circuit in the 1985-86 season. Among her consistently high finishes were a first place in super-G at Furano, Japan, and second in downhill at Badgastein, Austria. In 1987 Savijarvi won the downhill in the Canadian Championships at Rossland, British Columbia. She curtailed her racing career after sustaining knee and back injuries at the end of the 1987 season.

In February 1985 Chuck and Joyce Brooker were near the end of a two-day drive to Aspen for a ski vacation. As they approached Aspen they became increasingly preoccupied with the fortunes of their son Todd, who was competing in the World Cup downhill at Furano, Japan, the first World Cup event to be staged in that country. Anxious to know the outcome, they phoned ahead to the Aspen radio station and asked who

Todd Brooker in action at Panorama. – Courtesy: National Alpine Ski Team

had won. The man who answered the phone replied that it was "some Canadian." Excited by the news, they pressed him for the name. The radio station employee excused himself, then returned. "Some guy named Bricker. Yeah, Brooker, that's it," he replied when prompted by Chuck, who was by this time beside himself with excitement. Such are the anxieties and joys of being parents of a World Cup downhill champion.

Todd Brooker started skiing at the age of four. He was born into an athletic family. His father, Chuck, had been a hockey player with the Kitchener-Waterloo Dutchmen and carried Canadian colours at Cortina d'Ampezzo in the 1956 Winter Olympics. His mother, Joyce, was an all-around athlete and, like her husband, came from a family of hockey players. Ironically, the Brookers were apprehensive about their sons Marc and Todd playing hockey, as they feared injuries. When Todd was four, all of the Brookers began skiing, and the whole family took advantage of free ski lessons at the Devil's Glen resort. Then they joined the Toronto Ski Club and faithfully journeyed to Blue Mountain every winter weekend from their home near Waterloo. They had no chalet, so they returned home each Saturday night and came back again on Sunday morning.

In 1969 nine-year-old Todd caught the attention of Rudy Hiegelsberger, head coach of the Toronto Ski Club racing program. Rudy had immigrated to Canada from Austria, where he had been a junior racer and apprentice cabinetmaker. An ace downhill and slalom racer, he had competed in the Quebec Kandahar with a cast on one of his legs. After a brief venture in founding his own ski resort near Toronto, Rudy was recruited by Jozo Weider in 1967 to become the ski school director. When Ernie McCulloch took over two years later, Rudy was able to concentrate on developing a junior racing program at the Toronto Ski Club. He recruited young skiers right off the hill and soon had them following him over bumps and through gates.

Rudy's method with his young charges on the Nancy Greene team was not to overburden them with theories or too much verbal instruction. He made their practice sessions enjoyable and guided his team over a variety of terrain, frequently at high speeds. "We skied and skied with Rudy," remembers Todd Brooker. "We usually did at least 25 runs a day." Rudy recalls Todd as an exuberant youngster, with an unruly mop of red hair, a boy who fearlessly schussed behind him down the newly cut Calamity Lane on the Apple Bowl. At Osler Bluff he won his first major downhill wearing blue jeans after he failed to find a racing suit that would fit. Joyce Brooker was watching along with Rudy Hiegelsberger and remarked in alarm: "He doesn't seem to be going very fast." "Don't worry," replied Rudy, "he's smooth." Todd was already exhibiting the gliding ability that helped him win so many downhills, along with his technical skills on the hard icy pitches.

A young Todd Brooker, 1984. – Courtesy: National Alpine Ski Team

The Blue Mountain team in the Todd Brooker Ski Challenge, March 1990. Left to right: Don and Helen McGillivray, George Weider, Andrea and Gord Canning. – Courtesy: Blue Mountain Resorts Limited

Todd's aggressiveness and tenacity in training soon paid off in winning race times, and he progressed to the Southern Ontario Division and to his first national win, the Canadian Junior Downhill Championship in 1975. From there he went on to the National Alpine Training Squad in 1977 and to the National Alpine Team in 1979. This was the start of his 10-year career as a Crazy Canuck. Launching this career was a struggle at first. He was almost marooned in Toronto when the CSA informed his parents that there were no funds to send him to Europe. The Brookers informed Gordon Canning of the situation and the necessary $2,000 was quickly contributed by a joint effort involving Blue Mountain Resorts, the Toronto Ski Club (headed by Michael Davies), and Chuck and Joyce Brooker. Todd was hampered by a knee injury that forced him to sit out the 1979-80 season and curtailed his progress in 1980-81. Then he amazed the Europeans by breaking into the top 10 in 81-82 to become a leading contender on the World Cup circuit. The following year he dazzled the ski world with wins at Kitzbuhel and Aspen.

Rudy Hiegelsberger was on the scene at the Kitzbuhel race and made a major contribution by persuading his former pupil to enter. Todd had been favouring a bruised shin and was not planning to participate. Rudy suggested that he reconsider, as this would be a situation where nobody expected him to do well and the pressure would be off. Todd followed this advice and his run on the formidable *Hahnenkamm* became his first World Cup win. The *Hahnenkamm* is the most prestigious ski-racing event in the world, and Todd's victory there was the one most treasured by his family, with the Japan title placing a close second because of the spectacular reception accorded him by the Japanese. One of Todd's proudest possessions is a huge, ornately embossed Samurai warrior's helmet, one of the many gifts he received after his victory in Japan.

In a sense it was fitting that Todd ended his career on the *Hahnenkamm*, the last Crazy Canuck to hang up his helmet. In February 1987, as 60,000 spectators lined the course, he endured a terrible cart-wheeling crash only yards from the finish line. After five days in the hospital Todd was flown home, where he enjoyed a long rest and announced his retirement from competition. In spite of his pain and dizziness he insisted on writing thank-you notes almost immediately to the many well-wishers who had written him.

Todd's 10 years on the World Cup circuit brought him fame among the fanatical European fans of the sport, as well as national recognition at home. He learned German, and his genial and outgoing personality made him an ideal spokesman in a sport that the Canadians broke into so suddenly and unexpectedly. He was greatly admired for his tenacity in refusing to succumb to his many injuries and his fearlessness in pushing himself to the limit of his abilities. These attributes served him well in his pursuit of a business career in ski promotion and hotel development. He now resides at Blue Mountain with his wife and newly born twin daughters, and is in charge of the Todd Brooker Lodge, currently being built on the ground previously occupied by Jozo's Blue Mountain Lodge at the north edge of the resort. Todd also oversees the Todd Brooker Ski Challenge, a benefit celebrity race at Blue Mountain that has become an annual event and which raises $125,000 each year for the Ronald McDonald House for children suffering from cancer. Although he favours his severely injured leg, with almost no feeling between the knee and the ankle, Todd is a fierce competitor on the tennis courts and golf course at Blue Mountain.

A Four-Seasons Resort

As the Blue Mountain operation grew in scope there developed an urgent need to generate revenue during the non-winter months and to create a year-round resort community that would make Blue Mountain the centre of that community's activities. Toward this end, over the course of the resort's history a number of attempts were made to develop a cultural centre.

At the beginning of the 1950s Jozo built a stage beside the Ski Barn and ringed the hill behind the Barn with several hundred benches. He also had plans drawn up for a regular amphitheatre. He promoted the stage and organized several performances by major choirs and national ballet companies. This time the summer weather was against him. The performances were ruined by heavy rainstorms. Even on nights when the skies cleared, the ballerinas had trouble holding their footing on the rain-soaked plywood stage. Mosquitos swarmed out of the long, wet grass, tormenting the spectators and biting the scantily clad dancers. The performances were soon discontinued as a result of the considerable financial loss. "These were the most expensive ballet tickets that anyone could ever have bought," Jozo lamented after the fiasco was over. He had mortgaged the Weider farm to support the cultural experiment, but was able to recover from the failure and retain the property.

In 1974 Gordon Canning repeated Jozo's efforts in the musical arts, forming, with Toronto promoter Richard Stultz, the Blue Mountain School of Music. Students from the music school were housed in nearby Tyrolean Village and instructed by a first-rate faculty headed by Dr. Boyd Neel, a musician of international repute. Hotel guests and local chalet owners were treated to evening concerts by students and faculty members in the Base Lodge. While the setting was informal, Boyd Neel was a perfectionist and took the public performances very seriously. When four-year-old Andrea Canning, Gordon's daughter, wandered near the podium during a recital by a chamber ensemble that Neel was directing, he stopped the performance with a flourish of his baton and solemnly intoned in his stentorian Oxford accent, "Will someone please remove the offending infant."

With the assistance of a grant from the Ontario government, a concert shell was built beside the Base Lodge. Jazz and classical performances and major bluegrass festivals were held in the shell before several thousand spectators seated on the hillside. Among the big-name performers who appeared were jazz flautist Moe Koffman and Paul Hoffert, leader of Lighthouse. As in the case of Jozo's efforts, the music school had to be abandoned bacause it proved unprofitable. However, it did have a permanent impact on the Collingwood and Blue Mountain communities, giving rise to the Blue Mountain Foundation for the Arts. Energetically directed for several years by Barbara Weider, the Foundation became a permanent institution which has organized concerts and other cultural events, published books, and arranged lectures and speeches on artistic and literary topics.

A Music School student tuning up in preparation for a performance, 1975.
– Courtesy: Blue Mountain Resorts Limited

The problem of how to extract money from the hills during the summer had always been a puzzle that resisted a solution. After Jozo's unsuccessful experiment with concerts and ballet performances, he began operating a chairlift for summer visitors. Yet, although the ride was pleasant, there was nothing to do but admire the scenery, and the operation had only marginal success.

The Blue Mountain Symphony Orchestra, conducted by Paul Hoffert of Lighthouse, with guest soloist Moe Koffman on flute, play the Blue Mountain Concerto I, during the official opening of the Concert Shell, August 9, 1975.

– Courtesy: Blue Mountain Resorts Limited

A 12-hour marathon, the Collingwood Pepsi-Cola Bluegrass Festival and Five-String Banjo Contest featured the Good Brothers; Cement City; Edward, Harding & McLean; Denis LePage, World's Champion Five String Banjo Picker in 1976, and his band Station Road; Rudy Meeks; and more, August 1981. – Courtesy: Blue Mountain Resorts Limited

The installation of the Great Slide Ride marked the arrival of Blue Mountain's first major summer attraction.
– Courtesy: Blue Mountain Resorts Limited

In 1975 Blue Mountain was approached by John Clifford, who was managing the Mt. Cascade ski resort near Ottawa on behalf of a foreign owner, Freiherr (Baron) Karl von Wendt. A polished aristocrat with a good head for business, the baron had built a ski resort in Germany on ancestral lands owned by his family. During a time when his resort was floundering due to mild winters, he formed the concept of a summer ride based on a cement track running down the mountain. When he proposed the plan to some technicians, they advised him to go to a psychiatrist and get treatment for mental illness. Finally he persuaded an engineering company to make a prototype of the track. At a grand opening at the baron's resort, with many reporters and photographers on hand, the first riders descended on mats made out of pieces of carpet. But the mats were uncontrollable and the riders slithered off the track and crashed into the surrounding forest. Shaken but still determined, the baron turned the problem over to designers at the Porsche automobile factory, who devised a sled with retractable wheels that could be easily controlled and even braked to a halt if necessary. With the help of engineers, Von Wendt constructed a winding track with high-banked turns to make the ride a thrilling but relatively safe attraction.

Von Wendt perfected the slide ride on home ground in Germany and then made arrangements for manufacturing in North America. He built the first Canadian slide at Mt. Cascade, and with Clifford's help was attempting to introduce it to other ski resorts. The baron flew to Toronto to meet the Blue Mountain directors, and speaking in flawless English he persuaded them to give the operation a try. The details of the $500,000 deal were worked out in an all-night negotiating session involving the baron's Canadian agent, Al Rotenburger, Gordon Canning, myself and Blue Mountain's Collingwood lawyer, Bob Thompson. Toward morning both parties were utterly exhausted and inclined to compromise, and the transaction was completed. The Great Slide Ride, as it was called, was an instant success and anchored summer operations year after year.

Much needed in the area were better hotel accommodations. Michigan skier Bob Charlton recalls arriving at 11 on a Friday night in the winter of 1968, after a five-hour drive from Detroit, and being locked out of the Blue Mountain Inn, where he had reservations. The night man had grown tired of waiting and had gone home. Charlton and his party were directed by the police to a derelict motel in Craigleith, where a sleepy attendant in a nightcap and nightshirt wordlessly handed them a key to

The new Inn Café addition and the original Blue Mountain Inn nestle at the bottom of the Inn Triple Chair, winter 1975.
– Courtesy: Blue Mountain Resorts Limited

George Weider, President of Blue Mountain Resorts Limited, and Claude Bennett, Minister of Industry & Tourism, officially open the Great Slide Ride, July 14, 1977.
– Courtesy: Blue Mountain Resorts Limited, Credit: Owen Sound *Sun-Times*

The original Blue Mountain Inn, c. 1972. Constructed in 1961, it was replaced by a 100-room hotel complex in 1981.
– Courtesy: Blue Mountain Resorts Limited

their room. Bob had hardly settled into bed when he was startled by an agonized shriek from Mrs. Charlton. She had been pinched by a crack in the toilet seat. She also complained that the mirror in the bathroom was only three inches square and was attached to the wall by a Band-Aid. In the morning they drove to Blue Mountain and were welcomed by Jozo, who apologized profusely for their mistreatment and charmed them into staying for their ski week instead of returning home as they planned.

After 1975 accommodations in the Blue Mountain area were co-ordinated in a central reservations system belonging to an association of hotel owners, the Blue Mountain Lodging Association. It was organized by Gordon Canning, Bev Taylor and Joe Kablinger, and run from the Blue Mountain offices. Later it was managed by the Georgian Triangle Tourist Association, based in Collingwood. Blue Mountain upgraded its own hotel facilities. In 1981 the new 100-room Blue Mountain Inn was built at a cost of $5.5 million on the site of the 20-room inn that had served as the resort's accommodations centre since 1962. The facilities included meeting rooms, saunas, an indoor swimming pool, and squash and racquetball courts. The five-star hotel was a monumental improvement over the old inn and firmly established Blue Mountain's status as a year-round destination resort.

While Blue Mountain and the Collingwood area have been known primarily as a winter vacation destination, summer activities have become important during the last 15 years. This is reflected in the style of the chalets, which are much bigger and more luxurious; they are designed for year-round use, and, for some, full-time residency upon retirement. The Cranberry Village and Rupert's Landing developments offer marinas and beach access as part of their recreational facilities. In 1981, when Blue Mountain built its hotel and conference centre, it also acquired 700 feet of sandy beach, which was made available for guests in the hotel and the surrounding condominiums. The Blue Mountain beach is an ideal spot for board-sailing, whose popularity has mushroomed in recent times. Steady breezes and sandy beaches make the Georgian Bay shoreline at Craigleith ideal for the sport. The waters off Northwinds Beach opposite the Depot Restaurant are teeming with sails on most summer days.

The finest beach in the Georgian Triangle area is at Wasaga. In 1984 Blue Mountain ventured beyond its home base at Craigleith and built a water slide in the heart of the tourist area in Wasaga Beach. This summer operation, in which $1.3 million has been invested, is managed by Blue Mountain's versatile Ski School Director, Ron Westlake.

After 1977, when the installation of the Great Slide Ride launched the resort into summer recreation, Gordon Canning and his management team began scouting around for attractions that would be complementary. An ideal companion attraction was found in the Slipper Dipper Waterslide, which was built next to the Slide Ride in 1980 at a cost of $700,000. Five years later an additional $300,000 was invested in another water-based attraction, the Tube Ride. The three slides, one dry and two wet, represent an investment of nearly $2 million and draw over 300,000 visitors each summer to the resort.

The counterpart to Blue Mountain's massive winter recreation complex is the recently completed Monterra golf course, which has beautified the resort and given it a strong anchor in its line-up of four-seasons vacation opportunities. Monterra is a result of more than 10 years of planning by the resort's management. The land for the golf course and accompanying housing development was assembled by real-estate entrepreneur John Kadwell in 1972. With Blue Mountain he formed a development company which acquired 380 acres between the mountain and the bay. Toronto golf-course designer Tom McBroom was hired by Blue Mountain and immediately saw the possibilities offered by the site. It offered a pleasing variety of terrain and vegetation, with natural gradations provided by ravines, creek beds and the gently sloping tablelands of a mini-escarpment that drops off to a flatland northeast toward Georgian Bay. McBroom's intent was to incorporate the look and feel of the escarpment – the backdrop to the site – into the course itself.

McBroom, Canning and part of the Blue Mountain management group visited Florida to study golf courses and were attracted to Grand Cypress, which had been designed by Jack Nicklaus. Nicklaus's trademark was the undulating mounds that set off the borders of the fairways. The Florida trip and Grand Cypress provided the inspiration for McBroom and the Blue Mountain group. McBroom adapted the concept of the mounds with great sensitivity to the Monterra site, shaping the mounds in a way that seemed natural to the setting. Each mound could be considered a small-scale replica of the mountain itself. The setting and the layout were especially suited for housing projects. An 83-lot subdivision was developed in the northeast section of the course, and additional housing is planned.

Ron Heesen, previously with the Toronto Board of Trade, was hired as Director of Golf and worked with McBroom and Evans Construction to prepare the soil and implement the design. Under McBroom's guidance the outer edges of the mounds were planted with red fescue, a coarser grass that, together with the mounds, gives Monterra a distinctively Scottish appearance: appropriate in view of the fact that Craigleith was settled mainly by people of Scottish origin. The reedy fescues adorn the mounds with a delicate straw colour. Waving in the summer breezes, they offer a pleasant contrast to the meticulously manicured bent grass of the putting greens. No expense was spared by Canning and Heesen to maintain the quality called for by McBroom's design; an expenditure of nearly $3 million was required to complete the project.

As designed by McBroom, the Monterra golf course is a par 72 with a length of 6,581 yards. The course was opened in the summer of 1989 and immediately began receiving rave reviews. Golfers found it challenging without being formidable. Demanding holes such as Fortitude (No. 5), a long par-four at the bottom of a commanding bluff from where the tee-off is made, are followed by easier par-three holes for relief. The linked fairways, protected by the mounds, provide a feeling of intimacy and concentration when playing each hole. Hole No. 6 is called Lake Nipissing after the post-glacial lake that used to cover the lower section and whose lake shore formed part of the mini-escarpment. It is a par-three with its own small lake between the tee and the green. The final hole (No. 18) is named Algonquin after the great glacial lake that once covered Southern Ontario. It has two of the bigger water hazards on the course, twin lakes that also act as a reservoir for snowmaking. A spectacular view is afforded by Stagefright, hole No. 10. The tee is on a bluff overlooking the green and a ravine with a fast-flowing creek. In springtime trout can be seen in the stream. Another beautiful hole is Silver Creek (No. 14), named for the nearby tributary of one of the major creeks in the Craigleith area.

Gordon Canning's favourite hole is Mountain High, No. 16 returning to the mountain. "You look at the mountain in a variety of lighting and colour each time you play," he says. Golf authority Arthur James wrote, "The Ski Slopes serve as a backdrop for a green surrounded by mounding like meringue on a lemon pie." In reviewing the course soon after its opening, he added, "This course will certainly rate as one of the golf challenges in Canada."

Blue Mountain People

So many men and women have been engaged in tasks like trail-cutting, pipe-welding, cooking and serving meals at Blue Mountain over the 50 years that it would be impractical to render a comprehensive account of their labours on the front lines of the resort. However, the stories of Larry Plater and the Sheridan family are especially interesting because of their historic connection with the resort and the area.

One of machinist Larry Plater's most ambitious undertakings was taking apart and rebuilding the massive gear box from the Tranquility Chairlift. "Anything that breaks around here, I get to fix," he says, summing up his many duties in the resort's machine shop and garage. Weighing five tons, the gear box is so massive that the roof of the lift building had to be taken off in order that it could be removed by a crane.

Larry was born in Collingwood in 1948 and has lived all of his 42 years at the foot of Blue Mountain. He was educated in the one-room school in Craigleith and at Thornbury High School. Platers have always been abundant in Craigleith. Larry's great-grandfather Henry Benjamin Plater came to Craigleith from Toronto in the 1870s. "I was told that he was a shoemaker and later a horse trader," says Larry. "It might have been through his horse-dealing that he got the land that my family farmed here."

Much of the land owned by the famous Fleming family ended up in the hands of the Platers, and Larry spent part of his youth in the house built by Sir Sandford Fleming for his father, Andrew Grieg Fleming. When Larry was ready to start his own family in 1972, he moved out and built a new house on an adjoining lot. The Fleming house had been built almost 100 years earlier. A handsome Victorian building about halfway between the mountain and the bay, it was not only the Fleming home, but also served as Craigleith's post office in the early years. Larry's father sold the property to a developer, who demolished the historic home with a bulldozer in 1989. "One of the doors in our house had Sir Sandford Fleming's signature on it," Larry remembers. The Platers' landholdings were extensive, stretching almost to Georgian Bay on the north and including part of the mountain to the south. Larry's father, Buster, and his uncle Cecil owned the slopes between the Apple Bowl and the O-Hill before selling their farms to Jozo near the end of the 1950s.

Larry represents the third generation of his family that has worked for the resort. His grandmother Myrtle cooked for Jozo in the Blue Mountain Lodge in the 1940s. She also accommodated skiers in her farmhouse. In the 1940s they paid $5 per night for lodging and two meals. His father collected entrance fees for Jozo at the Gatehouse. His aunt Marcella was an outstanding Ontario ski racer at the end of the 1940s and has worked for the resort from time to time, most recently in the ski rentals department. Among the family mementos there is a badge with the inscription "Blue Mountain Police" that was once worn by Larry's father. The exact origins of this item are unknown, but it may be surmised that Jozo invented his own police force for coping with the difficulty of stopping cars on the public road in order to collect the entrance fees.

Blue Mountain machinist Larry Plater with gear box from the Tranquility Chair. – Courtesy: Larry Plater

As a teenager Larry worked for the resort during summers, picking stones off the new trails that were being prepared around the central part of the area. Later he drove backhoes and grooming vehicles. But his real love was always tinkering with machinery, and from a young age he was

Ron Sheridan began his career as a lift operator on the Red Devil in 1948 and switched to the North Poma in 1955. He was on hand for the official opening of the North Chair in February 1966 and served there until 1989. Standing left to right: Bill Skelton, Art Horner, Ron Sheridan, Keith Neil, Ken Skelton and Jozo Weider.
– Courtesy: Jack MacMurchy,
Credit: Fritz Schuller

taking machines apart to see how they worked. "I wasn't satisfied with the knowledge I got in high school," he says. "They taught mainly general arts, while my interests were technical." He has undertaken his own technical education, completing numerous courses in his spare time. On the walls of his machine shop are certificates indicating his qualifications as a construction millwright, compressor operator, and heavy-duty equipment mechanic.

Since becoming a full-time employee of the resort in 1967, Larry has applied tender care to thousands of bearings, wheels, pulleys and the various moving parts of equipment in lifts, backhoes and grooming vehicles. Working with Czechoslovakian-born welder Tony Posta he has fabricated the chairs, towers, and wheel assemblies of most of the lifts on the mountain. Supervised by Bill Skelton, the two have carried on the tradition of self-sufficiency begun by Jozo and Bill's father, Ken, who retired in 1978.

Aubrey and Ron Sheridan were born in their parents' farmhouse at Loree, near the top of the present Georgian Peaks resort. Until recently, when they sold their farms and moved into Thornbury, the two men carried on farming next to each other in the same location most of their lives. This was combined with concurrent careers as lift operators at Blue Mountain dating from the late 1940s.

Almost all of the Sheridan clan have been employed at the resort at one time or another. In the Sixties Ron's daughter Rhonda served food in the Höhenblick Café at the top of the South Chair during the summers. Her life was cut short when a recklessly driven car full of teenagers collided with hers on one of the roads near their farm. Her sisters, Carol and Bonnie, were ticket sellers. Ron's wife, Imogene, worked in the cafeteria at the Toronto Ski Club. Ron and Imogene's sons, John, Tom and Rick, are part of the Blue Mountain staff today. John supervises lift construction and recently assisted in the installation of the new quad chairlift at Tranquility. Rick is an electrician's apprentice. Tom operates one of the $150,000 grooming vehicles, manoeuvring it around the hills each winter night, chopping down moguls and churning the hard snow into powder. During the summer he operates a backhoe and small bulldozer and works on lift maintenance. Aubrey's son Rob does the same type of job. Two of Aubrey's sons, Terry and Doug, previously worked at Blue Mountain but now operate their own machine shop business.

The initiation of the two elder Sheridans to the resort was a rough one. They were posted in front of Jozo's Gatehouse and instructed to collect the very unpopular guest fee from skiers entering the resort who were not members of the ski clubs. Ron was collecting fees in front of the Gatehouse when a policeman came along and told him that it was illegal to stop cars on a public road. Sheridan went to Jozo to inform him of what had happened.

"Is the policeman still there?" asked Jozo.

"No, he's gone," Sheridan replied.

"Well, don't just stand there!" Jozo roared. "Go back out and start stopping them again."

Aubrey Sheridan regretted complaining about being too cold while parking cars, because Jozo promptly moved him into the Ski Barn to wash dishes. "There were mountains of them," he remembers. "There was no automatic dishwasher, and they all had to be done by hand. The job never seemed to end. I was glad to get back out to the lifts."

Jozo was a benevolent employer, but he could be volatile and unpredictable. Jozo fired Aubrey and promptly rehired him at least three times. On one occasion Aubrey was resting after some tiring work. At the end of each day of operation, the sleigh tow cable had to be elevated by blocks of wood that were placed under it on crests along the route where it cut into the ground. Otherwise the cable would freeze in the groove that it made while running, and it had to be shovelled out and pried loose. This tedious job had to be done if the operator forgot the propping assignment, which was often the case.

Members of the Sheridan family have worked at Blue Mountain since 1948. On staff in 1990 are, left to right, rear: Tom, Aubrey and Rick Sheridan. Left to right, front: John and Rob Sheridan.
– Courtesy: Blue Mountain Resorts Limited, Credit: Leslie Kamps

Aubrey and two workmates were taking a break in the hut at the bottom of the sleigh tow after working on the cable, when Jozo suddenly walked in and exploded. "You lazy devil – you're fired!" he told Aubrey. As Aubrey dejectedly picked up his lunch pail and prepared to walk down the hill, Jozo shouted, "Where are you going? Come back here." Aubrey was summoned back to the tow shed and given another 15-minute tongue-lashing, after which he was again taken on as an employee.

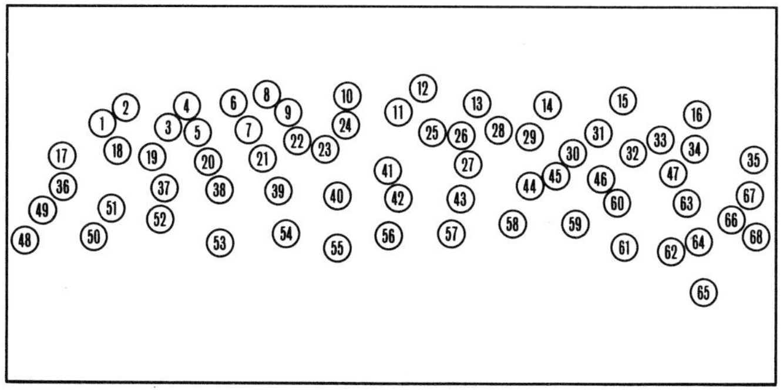

Blue Mountain Operations Staff, February 14, 1973. 1. Doug Reekie; 2. Dave Horner; 3. John McKean; 4. John Bell; 5. Harvey Carscadden; 6. Tom Sheridan; 7. Len Kennedy; 8. Eric Reekie; 9. Grant McMurchy; 10. Robbie Keith; 11. Bob Starrett; 12. Jim MacKay; 13. Larry Brownlee; 14. Orm Lougheed; 15. Bill Forsythe; 16. Tom Bellamy; 17. Bill Morrison; 18. Gary Ward; 19. Harold Reekie; 20. George Morrison; 21. Art Horner; 22. Frank Joyce; 23. Ron Sheridan; 24. Brian Ward; 25. Jerry Fararr; 26. Alex Cottrell; 27. John Currie; 28. Earl Fieghen; 29. Gary Carscadden; 30. Murray Taylor; 31. Brian Kennedy; 32. Lamont Waddell; 33. Harvie Reekie; 34. Doug Fieghen; 35. Little McDuffie; 36. Marshall Weatherall; 37. Ray Gardiner; 38. Aubrey Sheridan; 39. Rod Knott; 40. Larry Plater; 41. Elmer McNally; 42. Tom McGuire; 43. Allen McCulloch; 44. Chris Monaghan; 45. Aubrey Gallagher; 46. Gord Breadner; 47. Vern McGuire; 48. Bill Skelton; 49. George Weider; 50. Cliff Drake; 51. Elwood Thomas; 52. Allen Bath; 53. Wesley Dean; 54. Keith Dooks; 55. George Chaudet; 56. Tony Posta; 57. Karl Gerschwiler; 58. John Sheridan; 59. Les [???]; 60. Burton Lougheed; 61. Carman Hodgkinson; 62. Terry Sheridan; 63. Gord Canning; 64. Leo Low; 65. John Forsythe; 66. Alex McVicar; 67. Russell McDuffie; 68. Glyn Griffiths.

– Courtesy: Blue Mountain Resorts Limited

The brothers remember that at the end of a day's skiing the tow operators would each bring their tin cash boxes to the Gatehouse. The money would be counted and each employee paid right on the spot. If it was a profitable day, the operator might get $12; if the take was inadequate, he might have to settle for $8. "We did not complain," recalls Aubrey. "These were tough times and we were glad to get anything at all." "If the winter was good," notes Ron, "there would also be a bonus at the end of the season. When Jozo did not have enough money, we were paid in shares."

While working mainly winters, Aubrey and Ron also helped construct several lifts, including the North Pomalift. Many parts and tools had to be carried up the lift line by hand or dragged up with a team of horses. "We had to carry up oxygen tanks for the acetylene torches that were used to cut the arms on the towers," recalls Ron. "Each tank weighed over 100 pounds." A wooden tripod with a pulley was improvised for the erection of the lift towers, which were then pulled into place by the horses. Later a derrick was mounted on the old army truck to do this job.

When Jozo could not afford to put a new motor into his old Massey-Harris tractor, Ron brought his own tractor from Loree, and used it to power rope tows behind the Ski Barn and on the O-Hill. "Jozo was always trying out something new," Ron remembers. "He had me set up my tractor at the top of the O-Hill, on the theory that it was easier to pull skiers to the top rather than push them from the bottom. It worked all right. I was able to pull six skiers up the hill, while at the Ski Barn, my tractor would only allow four at a time. I had to sit in the unheated cab of my tractor. There was always a wind on top of the O-Hill and I was chilled to the bone."

From loading the North Poma, Ron graduated to the North Chairlift that was built in its place. Over the years he grew to know hundreds of skiers by name. Along with his brother he developed an eagle eye for catching skiers without tickets. "You developed a sixth sense for skiers who were cheating," he recalls. "There was something about the way they looked at you that told you they did not have a proper ticket." He would nab the offender and have him expelled from the resort or arrested by the police.

Ron remained at his post until 1989, when he was stricken with multiple sclerosis. He bears his pain with the stoicism that is characteristic of the rugged farmers of the escarpment.

Aubrey put in a similarly long term at the Apple Bowl, starting with the rope tow there and moving on to the pomalift and, after that to the Apple Bowl Chair. He was soon back on the job after being temporarily sidelined by a heart attack and a by-pass operation in 1988. He has worked at Blue Mountain every winter weekend of operations since 1948. He currently mans the new quad chair.

While appreciating the conveniences of the new technology, the two older Sheridans have fond memories of the resort's earlier days when everyone knew each other. At the end of each winter, they recall, the staff of around 30 would gather in the Ski Barn. Jozo would cook a chicken dinner and then bring out the accordion, or Ken Skelton would play the fiddle, and the floors and beams would shake with an old-fashioned barn dance.

Hikers taking the "Petun Loop" of the Bruce Trail between Blue Mountain and Osler Bluff can view the ruins of the Osler castle. The palatial summer residence was constructed by Britton Bath Osler, an accomplished Victorian lawyer and member of the Osler family. He built the home in 1893, calling it "Kionontio," *meaning "top of the hill" in the Petun language. His hope was that the fresh air and splendid setting would bring solace and better health to his ailing wife. Unfortunately she died before she could enjoy the property, and it lapsed into disrepair and decay.*

– Courtesy: Collingwood Museum

PART VI

Blue Mountain's Neighbours

When Fritz Loosli, the Swiss ski pro who cut the first trails at Blue Mountain at the end of the 1930s, told local farmers that all of the two-mile area between Blue Mountain's log clubhouse and the O-Hill would eventually be formed into ski slopes, they reacted in disbelief and thought it a lunatic statement. Not only was Loosli's prediction fulfilled 20 years later when Jozo Weider expanded the resort, but since 1950, five other sections of the 14 miles of escarpment land between Georgian Peaks on the northwest and Devil's Glen on the southeast have also been developed into ski resorts.

Osler Bluff

Osler Bluff was the first private club to be formed. In January 1949 Bill Kingsmill and Struan Robertson were vacationing with their wives at Mt. Tremblant when each discovered that the other had been independently considering the concept of forming a private ski club. This led them to a search for possible sites to the south of the Blue Mountain Resort, culminating in the purchase of a 50-acre property from the Franklin family for $2,000, followed by leases and options on another 400 acres from Sanford Franklin and Garnet Wagner. They then launched an intensive campaign which produced 36 charter members who paid $100 each. During the winter of 1949-50 the operation consisted of one trail, which they had managed to cut, and the sparsely furnished and barely heated, abandoned Franklin farmhouse.

Slowly more skiers were cajoled into joining up, and by the spring of 1950 there were 93 members. Many of them volunteered to cut trails on weekends, and the first real run, the Wagon Trail (now known as the "S"), was ready for the 1950 season. Other trails followed: the Slalom Hill, Hell's Highway (later incorporated into the Rattler), and the Marshall Plan. Improvisational engineering by Bill Kingsmill, Dick Scrivener and Bill Kaufman produced the "Richard Harding Scrivener Four-Car Reciprocating Ski Tow" with a capacity of 32 skiers. The four carriages, each carrying eight skiers, were built by Kaufman Furniture and were originally based on wheels with rubber tires. When this proved unwieldy, they were mounted on sleigh runners. The device functioned effectively, attracting much admiration in the ski community and serving as a selling point for new members. The early Oslerites had to put up with rugged conditions: unploughed roads in the winter, mud to the hubcaps in the spring, and fires that destroyed several of the chalets. Under the supervision of architect-builder Peter Weld, the members renovated the Wagner farmhouse with "Teperman's Number 1 Wormy" lumber and used it as the club's base facility for 23 years, until it was destroyed by the "Great Fire" in 1978. A favourite place to stay overnight was the "Oberhangargurble," built by Peter Weld, David Cochran and Ashley Kilgour. This building accommodated people who worked on the hills, as well as friends who were building their own chalets.

By 1954 the club was still in search of its target of 300 members and struggling with financial problems. The crisis was eased when Furn Francis was able to persuaded a crusty bank manager to grant a loan of $30,000, but only after it was personally guaranteed by 10 members. Despite these precarious beginnings the club went on to become a successful and prestigious organization with a modern base lodge, chairlifts and snowmaking equipment. Many of the charter members are still very active and proud of the traditions that evolved over the years. Regrettably missing from the Osler scene are charter member and legendary secretary and organizer Katie Ronson, who died in 1979; founder, Struan Robertson, who died in 1982; and Lloyd Shaw, the local farmer who managed the outdoor operation until his death in 1986. Osler, today, has 1,000 members and a long waiting list. Its roster could well be considered a "Who's Who" of Toronto's financial and professional elite.

Several skiers who joined Osler distinguished themselves in competitions during the 1940s and 1950s. This group included Connie Sparrow, Barbara Sullivan, Scotty Firstbrook, Alec Jacobs, David Cochran, Don Esson and Michael Gee. A stand-out among this group was Jake Robbins, who won many Ontario downhills during the 1950s. Among the women, Greta McGillivray was especially talented. The daughter of a famous Danish gymnast, she did her early skiing around Caledon. Later she spent some time honing her abilities in the Laurentians. A gritty competitor, she won the Ontario Ladies "A" Championship two years in succession, 1956 and 1957. She was successful in numerous Quebec meets as well, winning the prestigious Taschereau downhill in record-breaking time in 1952.

Osler's Ski Jump Hill under construction, c. 1966. Left to right: Fred Clark (bulldozer operator), Scott Fennell, unknown, Lloyd Shaw (Osler superintendent).
– Courtesy: Jack MacMurchy, Credit: Lee Stephenson

Osler's "Richard Harding Scrivener Four-Car Reciprocating Ski Tow," c. 1955.
– Courtesy: Sue Boehm, Credit: Les Tucker

Future Osler member Eddie Creed demonstrates a gelandesprung, 1949. Left to right: Liam O'Brien, Alf Brenner, Burny Clark and Eddie Creed. – Courtesy: Dave Cochran

Osler Bluff Ski Club, the first private ski club at Collingwood.
– Courtesy: Jack MacMurchy, Credit: Fritz Schuller

Laurie Graham competes in the 1987 Husky Downhill at Nakiska.
– Courtesy: National Alpine Ski Team

Members of the private clubs on the escarpment played an important role in the administration of the Canadian Amateur Ski Association and the Southern Ontario Ski Zone. Especially active from the Osler side in this organizational work were Katie Ronson, Jake Robbins and Ian "Buck" Rogers (Rogers went on to found the Georgian Peaks resort). Osler's own racing program produced National Team members Derek and Lynda Robbins, Scott Hutcheson and Jack Creed. A family tradition was upheld when Robin Kingsmill, daughter of "Swedish veteran Retep Llimsgnik" (Peter Kingsmill) won the Ontario Womens Alpine Championship in 1970.

The pride of Osler in the 1980s was Laurie Graham, who did her early racing in the Nancy Greene League and then climbed to national successes and Olympic and World Cup competition. For 11 years she anchored the Canadian women's Alpine team in international competition, participating in three Olympic winter games. Like her male counterparts, the Crazy Canucks, she showed great courage and tenacity in braving difficult downhill courses and coming back from injuries. She won five World Cup downhills in the course of her career and made Canadian ski history with her 1984 win in the super giant slalom, the first victory by a Canadian in that event. In 1986 she was named Canada's female athlete of the year. She retired from racing in 1988 after missing a silver medal at the Calgary Olympics by three tenths of a second. In March 1990 her fellow club members at Osler held a surprise celebration in her honour and named a trail after her, calling it "Laurie's Bluff."

Craigleith

Just as the Fifties had spawned a new private club to the south of Blue Mountain, the Sixties saw the development of a neighbouring club to the north, the Craigleith Ski Club. The southernmost slope of the new club was the "V" Hill, familiar to Blue Mountain skiers although never owned by Blue Mountain. The Georgas brothers had used the "V" Hill for slalom practice, and in the spring, diehard skiers wishing to continue the season would climb to the top and ski down through the snowbanks accumulated at the edge of the tree line.

The story of Craigleith's development has been related in a work by Molly Main. According to Mrs. Main, the groundwork was laid in 1956, when, with the precedent of a successful private club (Osler) already established, a group led by Doug Bowie, Bruce Huntley, Wallace Newman, Gordon Peck, Donald Whamond and Edward Woolven began looking for good ski territory all over Ontario, but finally realized that nothing could equal the vertical on the face of the Blue Mountain. At a total cost of $5,000 they purchased 85 acres from farmers Lorne Plater and Dan Fleming. The founding members chose the name Craigleith for the new club, not only because it referred to the area at the foot of the mountain, but also because it was Scottish. There was a significant Scottish contingent that had skied in their home country as members of the Dundee Ski Club or the Scottish National Club from Edinburgh.

The Craigleith Ski Club received its letters patent in March 1958. The entrance fee was set at $200. There were 150 voting members when the second annual general meeting was held in 1959. Two rope tows and a lift – the first T-bar in Southern Ontario – were in operation by the winter of 1959. The upper of the two rope tows was a makeshift contraption powered by an old bread truck that was hastily roped down over wooden barn beams. The lower tow was operated from the cab of a CPR truck that Bowie had bought at a bargain price; he donated the box of the truck to the Bullock brothers, who used it as a chicken coop on their farm.

From the top of the "Sling Shot," as the T-bar was called, the early Craigleith skiers could descend old logging trails or head down Healey's Comet (the name honoured founding member Ron Healey), the Bowie (Doug Bowie), or take Scott's Cure (Brian Scott) to Musil's Ride. The latter was named after Cyril Musil, the Czech refugee who had single-handedly cut the first trail.

In 1960 the first chalets began to spring up on leasehold land at the foot of the mountain. The owners had to put up with animals that wandered onto their property from a nearby ranch; among the intruders were horses, goats and a Brahman bull. In its negotiations with Lorne

A spring social gathering, c. 1975. Left to right, rear: Nancy Hall, Bette Wilson, Dorothy Brown, Ruth Stokes, Jeff Lash, Tom Brown, Bill Stokes, Bill Wilson, Jim Hall, Gord Cummings. Left to right, front: Sue Lash, Jack Dawson, Jeff Brown, Tony Camisso, Irene Camisso, Tom Fox, Betty Dawson, Laura Fox, Harriet Cummings.
– Courtesy: Craigleith Ski Club

Plater, the club had been forced to grant grazing privileges for Plater's cattle, and when the roaming cows became a nuisance, Plater had to be paid off to get out of the cattle business.

An important step was made in 1967 when the club bought the 200-acre Goodchild farm for $210,000. The land purchase was accompanied by an expansion program that provided for a new lodge, chairlift and additional trails. Gord Cummings was appointed club manager in 1968, a post he held for almost 20 years. Craigleith continued to expand through the 1970s. New subdivisions were built between the foot of the hill and the Blue Mountain road, and several club members, including Jim Hall, Alistair Lessels and Peter Townsend, moved to the area and made their chalets their permanent homes. Among Craigleith traditions, one of the most pleasant is their annual men's day, when numerous storytellers stand up to tell a steady stream of jokes and anecdotes, many enhanced by the rolling brogues of Edinburgh and Dundee.

The club won many honours as a result of the strong racing program developed by Leo Vogrin, Christopher Nowakowski and Hans Von Alman. In 1968 Craigleith racer Graham Hess won the Canadian Junior Championship and subsequently became a member of the National Team. In 1967 and 1968 Craigleith juniors were victorious in the newly formed Nancy Greene League. Among the Craigleith Nancy Greeners were names that were to become very familiar in ski circles and sports headlines: Lynn Warll, future director of the Blue Mountain Ski School and TV commentator, and future National Team skiers Steve and Craig Podborski and Rob Safrata. The successes of Steve Podborski on the World Cup downhill circuit were so remarkable that they deserve some additional comments.

This Craigleith racing alumnus possessed exactly the right combination of technical ability, intellect, courage and competitive fire to become the most successful World Cup downhiller that Canada has produced to date. He became an earner of respectable wages on the World Cup tour after his first victory at Morzine-Avoriaz in 1979. While always a raw challenge, the 80-mile-an-hour journeys over the deadly *Mausfalle*, *Steilhang* and *Alte Schniesse* of Kitzbuhel's *Hahnenkamm* became as familiar to Podborski as a trip on the 401 to his home in Don Mills. He obtained the respect and awe of the Europeans not only by his stupendous wins but also by his ability to speak German and French, and by the patience and skill with which he handled the tiresome problems of being a celebrity. Retirement came after 80 World Cup races, thousands of kilometres of travel on twisting Alpine highways, two major operations to restore destroyed ligaments in his knees, and 10 years of an austere regime of lonely hotel rooms, early morning runs and mental preparations that required the concentration of a Zen practitioner.

The rewards, though financially not on a scale of a world-class hockey player, were considerable. He was named the Canadian male athlete of the year in 1981, became an officer of the Order of Canada, and was inducted into the Canadian Sports Hall of Fame and the Honour Roll of Canadian Skiing. Most important was his own sense of achievement in

Instructor Mary Warll and her aspiring student Steve Podborski, 1962.
– Courtesy: Jackie Podborski

Austrian Harti Weirather, Canadian Steve Podborski and Swiss Peter Mueller salute their downhill successes on Aspen Mountain. Podborski is the 1982 World Cup downhill champion. – Courtesy: National Alpine Ski Team

knowing that he had been the best World Cup racer over an entire season, the first North American (and the only one thus far) to do this, and the first North American to win a medal in an Olympic downhill (a bronze at Lake Placid in 1980). He applied the discipline that had brought success on the World Cup circuit to become an entrepreneur, ski promoter and supporter of the Olympic movement. His autobiography, written with Gerald Donaldson in 1987, is full of discerning insights on the personalities of fellow Crazy Canucks, the fine points of equipment preparation and racing technique, and the abilities that are necessary for victorious downhilling. He chronicles the drudgery of the journeyman racer, with his equipment and conditioning, the toil in the darkness before success, and the pressures attendant on victory and fame.

Alpine members, c. 1965. Left to right: Konnie Jakowidas, Ruth Moses, Anna Lisa Jakowidas and Helmut Moses. – Courtesy: Philip Durnford

Alpine

The origins of the Alpine Ski Club are slightly different from those of the other private clubs, in that it was founded by members of a travelling club. The Alpine Ski Club emerged from the North Toronto "Y" club near the end of the 1950s. It was founded by Frank Patterson, Fergie Ferguson, Erling Morris and Hans Kent. The majority of its members were single, and many of them were new immigrants from Australia, Great Britain, Austria and other lands. "Very few of us had cars," remembers Hans Kent, a key founder of both the club and the new resort. "Those with vehicles were expected to provide rides for the rest." Led by Kent, a group within the Alpine club decided that they, like Osler and Craigleith, would like to settle down on their own hill. A search was carried out for an appropriate site, with the criteria of at least 400 vertical feet and a lake at the bottom. After reviewing several possible sites they decided on a valley just north of Craigleith Ski Club, commanding a 700-foot vertical drop and a spectacular view of Georgian Bay. The property was being offered for sale by Max Campbell, who operated Arrowhead Ranch, a struggling equestrian resort. The site was very attractive, with the slopes nestled between two folds of the mountain and sheltered from the winds blowing off the bay.

There were 300 Alpine Ski Club members by the time Kent and his friends were ready to make their move to the Blue Mountain area. The majority of these members preferred to remain a travelling club, and they formed a new club which they called the "Voyageurs," signifying their intention to remain nomads. In its first season of operations on Blue Mountain, 1960-61, the Alpine club had only 119 memberships, 20 of them taken up by married couples who paid $150; the single membership was $100. "In 1960," remembers Kent, "so few people had the initiation money available that we had to arrange through our bank for them to get loans, and the loans were guaranteed by the club." In turn the founding members of the club had to guarantee a bank loan of $7,000 to fund the deficit encountered in starting up the operation.

The club leaders, assisted by volunteers, set about developing the property on Blue Mountain, and immediately began clearing trails and erecting rope tows under the direction of John Davies. They did all the work themselves during weekends, keeping costs to a minimum. Only $1,000 was originally budgeted for tows and trails. In 1960 they had two ropes operating, and one year later a third rope tow was added. Kent is proud of one innovation, the use of electric motors to power the ropes. A Hydro inspector was induced to come out to the hill and approve an installation on Christmas Eve 1960. They also invented a device which was a slight improvement over foot-packing of the hills. It was a wooden roller which was manoeuvred down the hill by skiers.

Base facilities were initially very primitive. It was considered a milestone of progress when a deluxe women's outhouse was built in 1962; it was wallpapered and had a large mirror. In 1969 construction began on the first clubhouse, replacing the leaky warming hut, the "Longhorn Café." In 1962 Alpine Ski Club built its first T-bar, and eight years later, in 1970, its first chairlift was installed. Alpine had much to celebrate when it held its 25th anniversary party and homecoming in 1986. From the original group of 119 members in 1960 the club grew to 1,000 voting members in 1990.

Like its forerunners, Alpine has enrolled a high proportion of prominent business executives, engineers and architects, lawyers, doctors and accountants. They have managed the operation well, maintaining financial strength by bringing in new members when necessary and installing up-to-date facilities. The installation of two quad chairlifts in 1988 gave Alpine the most modern uphill transportation of any of the private clubs.

Georgian Peaks

The Georgian Peaks resort was established in 1960. The main founder and proprietor was Ian "Buck" Rogers, a ski enthusiast, Bay Street lawyer and former racer with the University of Toronto. Although he already belonged to Osler, he was ambitious to do something on his own. Key participants, along with Rogers, were lawyer Terry Wardrop, investment counsellor John Rykert, and ski adventurer and navy veteran Ross Wilson. Two ski experts were recruited by Rogers and played a prominent role at the new resort: Bill Whalen, formerly with Mt. Tremblant and Blue Mountain, took over outdoor management; Hans Wieland, a former Austrian racer, headed the ski school and established a ski shop at the base of the mountain. Requiring an investment of about half a million dollars, Rogers' venture was the boldest and most ambitious of the resort projects launched on the escarpment. He persuaded a core of 120 skiing families, many of them his personal friends, to form a club whose members would be the primary users. However, unlike Osler Bluff and Craigleith, the Peaks was also operated as a commercial venture open to the public.

In contrast to the relatively slow and painful development of Blue Mountain over the previous two decades, a powerful new resort was quickly built on the steep face of the escarpment. A chairlift and T-bar served the challenging Thunder and Lightning Run, the intermediate Minute Mile and the gentler Champlain. An additional three chairs were built in the course of the development.

An interesting sideline to the Georgian Peaks story is the attempt, initially successful, to revive the ski trains which had run during the 1940s. Since it was located right next to the railway track, Georgian Peaks

Surfacing again. After numerous skiing and war adventures, Ross Wilson helped found Georgian Peaks in 1960. An 80th birthday celebration was held for him at the Peaks in March 1990. The survivor of towering Norwegian ski jumps, a disastrous ski accident, naval combat on two oceans and two sinkings (one by Japanese and the other by German bombs), he now lives in a quiet street in Mississauga. The walls of his living room are lined with books, and behind the staircase are framed photos of the five ships that he served on: a battleship (the mighty King George V*), two cruisers and two corvettes. He speaks in a gravelly voice and has an amused look in the china blue eyes that are set off by a ruddy face. He remembers that during the war all four Christmases were spent at sea, but has no regrets about any of his adventures. "It's been an interesting life," he remarks, with the understatement that is habitual in his descriptions of the odyssey that began on the hills of High Park, where he skied while he was a student at Upper Canada College in the 1920s.*
– Courtesy: Ross Wilson

Georgian Peaks sits on the steep face of the Niagara Escarpment, c. 1980. – Courtesy: Blue Mountain Resorts Limited

Hans Wieland, pro at Georgian Peaks, flying high in 1964. His ski tips narrowly missed the head of the photographer. – Courtesy: Jack MacMurchy

The 1961 Beehive Professional Giant Slalom winners' circle. Left to right: Stein Eriksen (winner), Anderl Molterer, Ernie McCulloch, Othmar Schneider, Toni Spiess and Christian Pravda. – Courtesy: Jack MacMurchy

was a natural destination for approaches by train. In 1963 Rogers, urged on by a Stayner train buff, Peter Oehm, was successful in persuading the CNR to restore train service for skiers, a service that lasted two seasons. The ski trains operated on Sundays from January through March 1964, delivering skiers right to the Peaks, and they were run again the following season. The train left Union Station at 8 a.m. and arrived at Georgian Peaks at 10:45. It was an efficient mode of travel, considering that skiers were dropped off at Stayner (Devil's Glen), Collingwood, and Craigleith (Alpine and Blue Mountain). The returning train left Georgian Peaks at 5 p.m. The combined ski and train ticket in 1965 for any of the four resorts in the arrangement was only $7.75 for adults and $5.90 for children.

In 1961 Georgian Peaks hosted Canada's first professional ski race, the Beehive Giant Slalom, which was sponsored by the St. Lawrence Starch Company. It drew numerous world-famous racers, including former Olympians Stein Eriksen, Christian Pravda and Toni Spiess. Canada's Ernie McCulloch competed as well. As Ross Wilson later pointed out, this was probably the most illustrious field of skiing greats ever assembled in one place on the North American continent.

The Georgian Peaks Club had an excellent racing program which produced National Team competitors Doug Leigh, Diana Gibson and Judy Crawford. World Cup racer Jim Kirby was also a graduate of the program, having developed his excellent slalom technique on the steep icy pitches of the Peaks. The Peaks was also home ground for the brother and sister combination of Brian and Karen Stemmle. Their first taste of competition was in club races in the early 1970s. Each of these talented downhillers won a first place in Nor-Am downhill standings and went on to represent Canada in World Cup racing. Both competed in the Olympics: Karen at Sarajevo in 1984, and Brian at Calgary in 1988. Brian was the Canadian downhill champion in 1987.

In spite of the heroic efforts of Rogers and subsequent owners, Georgian Peaks did not achieve financial success. In 1975 it was sold to developer Peter Lush, who in turn sold it to Blue Mountain in 1981. Blue Mountain President Gordon Canning negotiated the purchase with Lush and his partner, Buffy Valentini, also a real-estate entrepreneur. When they were separated by $50,000 after hard bargaining, Valentini, who had been silent throughout the discussions, exclaimed: "It's only $50,000; let's flip for it." Canning declined, and was able to buy the resort for $1 million.

Under the direction of Canning and operations manager Bill Skelton, the capacity of the snowmaking system was tripled at a cost of over $1 million and the base lodge was totally renovated and modernized. Even after these improvements, which cost more than $2 million, the Peaks

Karen Stemmle competing in the 1983 World Cup downhill at Mt. Tremblant. This event, won by Laurie Graham, was the first women's World Cup downhill to be held on Canadian soil. – Courtesy: National Alpine Ski Team

Brian Stemmle trains at Bad Kleinkirchheim, Austria, for the 1988 Olympic Games. – Courtesy: National Alpine Ski Team

The two skiers descending from the top of Georgian Peaks have a magnificent vista before them. Eight hundred feet below are the ice-covered waters of Georgian Bay. Beyond the tree line that defines the western edge of the ski trails are the lush farmlands and orchards of the Beaver Valley, and the town of Thornbury, flanked by the bluffs of the escarpment. – Courtesy: Blue Mountain Resorts Limited

failed to deliver satisfactory financial results, and in 1987 Canning negotiated the sale of the resort for $4 million to a group of investors led by Al Ulsred, Ken Kent and Mike Owen. They were able to successfully form a new private club, the fifth such club in the vicinity of Blue Mountain. In the course of the negotiations, financial support was being offered to the new club by the Toronto bond trader and tycoon Venard (Len) Gaudet. The freewheeling businessman was a member of Georgian Peaks and owned a chalet nearby. The possibility of his involvement in the new venture promptly exploded when Gaudet was investigated by the Ontario Securities Commission and ended up with his financial empire in ruins.

The seizure of Gaudet's chalet by his receivers caught the attention of business writer Diane Francis. In her column in the *Financial Post* she noted the number of financiers and famous people who frequented the Blue Mountain area and the fact that the name of Gaudet's firm (Osler) was the same as that of an elite private ski club. Topping it all off was the name "Bay Street," used for one of the runs at the Peaks. "Collingwood has arrived," she ironically observed. "It has class distinction, pedigree and scandal."

Devil's Glen

The Devil's Glen Country Club was founded by three men who had been top Southern Ontario racers in the 1950s: Michael Gee, Don Esson, and Red McConville. Gee and Esson were attracted to the spectacular glen while driving past it on trips to competitions at Beaver Valley. In the winter of 1962 they conducted explorations of the terrain on skis. When they encountered other ski tracks they became alarmed and decided to act. They speedily carried out a complex land assembly involving 11 parcels of land, after obtaining 30-day options under different names. They originally intended to acquire only 140 acres but ended up purchasing 500 acres for less than $50,000. They then formed the Devil's Glen Skiing Corporation and identified 30 names of potential members. At the top of the list was Red McConville, a well-connected businessman who was active in the London Ski Club. Not only did McConville join them, but he accelerated the recruitment effort, selling units of the corporation at $5,000 each and raising $25,000 in less than a week. At only a third of the way down the list of prospective members, they had $80,000 in hand and were able to get a bank loan for an additional $60,000.

That Gee and Esson had chosen the right site was proved to them in the spring, when they walked into the property with McConville from the highway and found that the saplings that they had cut down at snow level while exploring during the winter were still five feet tall. They immediately began clearing a roadbed into the resort, and in June they laid out runs for the bulldozers, using paint and string. Trails were prepared in the summer, and a partially finished base lodge, designed by Eb Zeidler, was up by the opening of the season. The group intended to sell tickets to the public, but Gee only had $2,000 allocated for publicity and advertising to promote the little-known area. He got a break when he was able to attract Tony Spiess, a former Olympic silver medallist and coach of the Austrian ski team. Gee had met Spiess while skiing at Aspen, and the two had become friends. Spiess came to Devil's Glen in 1963 to become head ski instructor and run the ski shop.

Terrific publicity was generated for Devil's Glen when it hosted the Beehive Giant Slalom in February 1963, attracting Stein Eriksen, Anderl Molterer, Christian Pravda and Tony Spiess, the latter having settled into his new position. The race course, which was forerun by Red McConville, was a challenging one, with the difficult Waterfall Trail testing even the professionals. The trail had been iced over the night before in order to cover the rocks that had been sticking out of the thin cover. Witnesses remember it as an event with many thrills, especially when the racers came hurtling over a cliff near the top of the Waterfall trail and had to make a precise air-borne turn to get through one of the gates.

A crowd of 9,000 was on hand for the event, which was shown from coast to coast by CBC Television. Each spectator was given a free ticket to come back and try the resort another day. They all came back, but only once. Many skiers who were lured to the resort by the publicity were so intimidated by the sight of the challenging Waterfall trail that they did not venture onto the hill from the parking lot.

After operating Devil's Glen as a public resort for three years with indifferent results, the four active directors, Michael Gee, Red McConville, Jim McLaughlin and Tom Lailey, converted the corporation into a private club, selling 200 memberships at $500 each. They had 200 members before the first snowfall of the 1967-68 season. "Red McConville became the first president," writes club historian Diane Crews, "and what had begun as a dream on the part of two skiers on their way to a race has become the little bit of heaven to all of us who ski there."

Osler, the first of the private ski clubs, has celebrated its 40th anniversary, and the others, with the exception of the new Georgian Peaks club, have been established for at least a quarter of a century. They have become important institutions in the area, with histories almost as venerable as that of Blue Mountain. They also have changed a great deal over the years. Amusing stories of their primitive beginnings are swapped at their annual "ski-around" week, during which time each club takes its turn hosting the others. The facilities are up-to-date, although not opulent. Like Blue Mountain, most of the clubs have introduced summer recreational facilities.

There are a number of advantages that membership is considered to bestow: the pleasant atmosphere of a small community of skiers, most of whom know each other by name (no club has more than 1,000 members); the short lift lines; opportunities to form friendships and business relationships; and, for families who are competition oriented, the top-level coaching and the races in interclub leagues. Newcomers pay a hefty price for these privileges, on the rare occasions when vacancies occur. Whereas the founding members of Osler, for example, had to be dragooned into putting up $100 for a membership in 1949-50, the initiation fee for that club was $20,000 in 1986. Similar levies have been charged by the other clubs.

The atmosphere of the clubs is very low-key in comparison to that of Blue Mountain, with its massive snowmaking, variety of runs and ample places of entertainment. In the three decades since Jozo built his first chairlift in 1960, Blue Mountain has also made a determined effort to eliminate one of the primary causes of the defection of some of its original patrons to the clubs: the long wait to get on the lifts. Lift lines at Blue Mountain now rarely exceed 10 to 12 minutes and are usually shorter. Blue Mountain must be an aggressive corporation and push adventurously into the future, while the clubs are in a position to enjoy the benefits of their pioneering efforts and the quiet ambience of their small resorts.

The Blue Mountain executive group, 1990. Left to right: Dale McNichol, Vice-President Hotel, Restaurants and Condominiums; Harold Abbotts, Vice-President Finance; George Weider, Chairman of the Board; Gordon Canning, President; Bev Philp, Vice-President Marketing and Bill Skelton, Vice-President Operations.
– Courtesy: Blue Mountain Resorts Limited, Credit: Dan McCracken

PART VII

Blue Mountain Today and Tomorrow

Blue Mountain Resorts today is still a family controlled enterprise, and in a sense even more so than when started by Jozo Weider. In 1986 the company went private, purchasing the 22 percent of the common shares which were owned by outside shareholders. The reasoning behind the privatization was that the small position held by the public did not offer an advantage in terms of providing significant equity capital and at the same time caused cumbersome reporting requirements and observance of securities regulations. A large number of the minority shareholders had sat with their investment for decades and now wanted to cash in. The matter was put to a vote, and proxies representing majority of the shares were cast in favour of the "going private" transaction. The company redeemed 35,000 shares from 127 shareholders at a fair market value of $46.50 each, for a total cost of $1.6 million. The assumption of 100-percent control has been an advantage to the directors and managers, affording greater flexibility, both in corporate strategy and operational decision-making.

Privatization meant that the Toronto Ski Club had to give up its historic role as a shareholder in Blue Mountain Resorts. However, it did obtain considerable financial benefit from the transaction, selling its eight-percent holding for almost $600,000. Throughout its involvement with Blue Mountain, which by the late 1940s had become its main interest, the Toronto Ski Club did not seek to own and control the resort in the manner of the private clubs which arose on the escarpment. Rather, it played a supportive role in assisting Blue Mountain Resorts to develop the ski area. In some ways this was a disadvantage, but it also had its rewards. The club has been able to maintain its own enclave and retain important privileges within Ontario's most highly-developed resort. The TSC clubhouse, built in 1960, has been a focal point of the north area and the community. Throughout the 49-year relationship the club and the company have had to find a compromise between the demands of a commercial operation and the requirements of a non-profit organization dedicated to recreation for a restricted group of skiers. While the diverse objectives made a certain degree of conflict inevitable, both in Jozo's time and after it, the relationship has been a constructive one, and both organizations have been able to play a vital role in the development of skiing in Ontario.

In the half-century of its existence Blue Mountain Resorts has grown into a substantial corporate enterprise with a diversity of operations. Over 500 people are employed by the company at peak times during the winter, and a core of 175 full-time employees is maintained. In the 1940s and 1950s workers like Aubrey Sheridan were greeted by Jozo, who gave them instructions when they reported for work on a weekend day and paid them cash when the tows closed. The operation is now departmentalized, with an extensive computer system for record-keeping and controls. A full-time personnel manager was recently hired to deal with employee concerns.

In addition to the executives recruited by Jozo, two new managers joined the company in the 1970s and have important positions today. Dale McNichol has been with the resort since 1975. A native of the area, he was educated at Ryerson and George Brown colleges and obtained experience in Toronto, Western Canada and the Caribbean before returning to Blue Mountain and joining the resort administration. As Vice-President of Hotel, Restaurants and Condominiums, he oversees a complete range of food services from fine dining to fast food, as well as liquor service in the bars and base lodges. He also directs the Blue Mountain Inn and the growing new field of condominium rentals and management. Bev Philp replaced Colin Chedore as marketing director in 1980 and became Vice-President of Marketing in 1983. This was in sharp contrast to her starting position as a hill hostess. After assuming the top marketing job, she directed her department in launching a host of creative projects to raise Blue Mountain's profile and give skiers a good time off the hills as well as on them. Recently, she has contributed to a community project that is significant in view of its relationship both to the historic role of the railway and the more recent emergence of the Blue Mountain area as a year-round resort area. This year she has led the fund-raising effort for the Georgian Trail, a 32-kilometre bicycle and hiking trail along the old railway track from Collingwood to Meaford. Bev's athletic family resides in a subdivision built by Jozo on Carmichael Crescent. Her son

Dean and daughter Dallas led the Collingwood Collegiate to its latest Ontario championship in 1990.

With the new managers on board, the modernization effort has continued at a whirlwind pace. Four new chairlifts were built in the 1980s: Easy Street, a beginners' lift at the south edge of the Apple Bowl; a second chair at Blue Mountain North; the Voyageur beginners' lift on the Big Baby; and the Silver Bullet next to the Central Base Lodge. In 1990 a new beginners' lift will be built on the O-Hill. The extensive lift, hill-grooming, and the snowmaking facilities make Blue Mountain Ontario's largest ski resort and one of Canada's largest. The ski area takes up over 800 acres of escarpment land, on which there are 30 trails and 15 lifts. In 1985 the night skiing area was expanded to include Tranquility and the L-Hill. Six of the trails and four of the lifts have lighting for night skiing which has become increasingly popular in recent years, especially with local residents. In the 1989-90 season, 2,000 night season passes were sold.

In 1983 the cutting of six new trails began on the Apple Orchard, a 140-acre area on the south side of the developed part of the resort. The new trails can be reached by a trek from the top of the Big Baby Chair, but future plans call for their servicing with two new lifts and an extension of the snowmaking system to the south. The activation of the Orchard, with a capacity for 2,000 more skiers, will create the equivalent of adding a whole new ski resort to the Blue Mountain area. The resort, not including the Orchard, now has a comfortable capacity of 8,000 skiers. Especially in the past decade, the ski operation has evolved from a day skier area to a destination resort where extensive services are provided. The Blue Mountain Ski School employs over 100 qualified instructors and is based in two locations at the resort. The resort operates a day-care centre, winter and summer retail shops, and rental shops with 1,000 pairs of skis. The resort's marketing department has a staff of 15 and organizes 10 special events during the winter.

While the lands used for skiing are essentially the same as those acquired by Jozo in his first two decades, the layout of trails, the snow conditions and pattern of skiing have been revolutionized. The early trails cut by Fritz Loosli above the log clubhouse were only 30 to 40 feet wide; the ground underneath the snow was rough, and if any packing was done it was accomplished by skiers tramping up and down the hill. The smooth, wide-open slopes of today are manicured by a fleet of grooming vehicles. Surface lifts – rope tows, pomalifts and T-bars – have been replaced by chairlifts, allowing a safer, easier ride up the hill and freeing up more land for skiing. Whereas the Red Devil carried nine skiers up the Schuss, the Silver Bullet, a new detachable quad chair on Tranquility, with a ride that lasts three minutes, carries 2,600 skiers per hour.

Blue Mountain's massive snowmaking system, in which $5.5 million has been invested, is a reminder that the resort is in the high-tech age. There are 26 miles of steel pipe buried beneath the frost line, and 357 snow guns. At the end of the 1970s there was still one significant area, Blue Mountain North, that was not included within the snowmaking system. This was remedied in 1988, when snowmaking was extended to the North Area. Ninety-six percent of the area served by lifts can be covered by man-made snow, with only the old Kandahar trail, originally cut around 1936, lying out of reach of the system. Water for snowmaking is pumped into an air-compressing station from three lakes linked together and holding a total of 45 million gallons. A sophisticated computer system is used to provide the proper air-water ratios, and in 1989 the snowmakers began using products of advanced biological engineering, injecting a protein enzyme into the water at the pumping station. Bill Skelton believes that this has made the system 25 to 30 percent more efficient.

While snowmaking and the new technology make the ski operation a more secure one than in the days of Jozo Weider, the management and staff, who have been effectively led by Gordon Canning since Jozo's death, will face many challenges in the next 50 years. The skier market has levelled off from the rapid growth rate (around 12 to 15 percent) of the 1960s and early 1970s. The aging of the population has reduced the segment that produces the most active skiers, the 18 to 35 year olds. The market opportunities are still significant, however. There are over a million skiers in Ontario today, and the fact that older people are more active seekers of recreation and exercise than in previous decades may offset some of the attrition that has been predicted by demographers.

Whatever the problems, the resort has enormous advantages because of its commanding position in the province's skier market and the development of year-round business, which has been quite pronounced in recent years. Although skiing and ski-related activities generate about two-thirds of Blue Mountain's revenue at this time, the resort has been successfully diversifying its operations over the other three seasons and finding markets where there is higher growth, such as golf. The resort's infrastructure is extensive and is being utilized year-round. More than 2,000 guests can be seated in the dining rooms and lounges of the Inn, the two base lodges and the new sports building. Since the mid-1970s, liquor regulations have been more reasonable, and the resort's entertainment business has become an important source of revenue. Particularly in recent years, however, caution has had to be exercised because of concern about alcohol and driving.

The installation of the Great Slide Ride in 1977 was a turning point for the resort, preparing the way for the property's move to year-round recreational operations. The thrust into summer activity was continued by the construction of the five-star Blue Mountain Inn and the acquisition of the beach near Georgian Peaks. Between 1986 and the present, 200 condominiums have been constructed and sold in the vicinity of the Inn and the Central Base Lodge. The condominiums have more than tripled the accommodations complex as a result of a rental program which manages the condominiums on behalf of the owners when personal use is not required. With the opening of the Monterra golf course and the new indoor tennis facility in 1989, vacationers, condominium owners and conference guests now have a complete line-up of recreational opportunities to enhance their enjoyment over the 12 months at the resort. The new $4-million clubhouse and recreational building, the Monterra Pavilion, is expected to be the nucleus of the resort village that is taking shape in the vicinity of the snowmaking lake and the Central Base Lodge. In the long-term plan are a 200-room hotel, additional condominiums and a commercial complex of offices and shops.

All of this would have impressed Jozo Weider, were he alive to witness the extensive utilization of the resort lands that he accumulated over 30 years with such great effort and financial risk. However, he may not have been totally surprised, as much of what has happened represents a fulfilment of his prophecies and his dreams for Blue Mountain.

Afterword

The writing of this book has caused me to relive many memories and reflect on a great many themes. The vagaries of history brought my family to Blue Mountain, and caused me, for a time, to take up history as my profession. While the teacher at our one-room schoolhouse in Craigleith was busy with the eight other grades, I thumbed through the dozen books that made up the school's library. My attention was caught by an illustrated history of the Bible, with its tales of the ancient Israelites and their battles. After that I discovered Russian literature on long winter nights at the resort, and my father gave me his own unpublished novel that he had written about his boyhood in Czechoslovakia. How he found time to write a 300-page book while building a ski resort and a major industry is something that mystifies me to this day! We worked on polishing his English, which was surprisingly good, considering it was not his native language. The intellectual journey that began this way took me through two universities and culminated in a teaching job at York University.

The sudden death of Jozo in 1971 removed me from my safe academic harbour and plunged me back into the world of business, where I had helped my father when he was farming, cutting trails, building lifts and founding his pottery business. While this move put serious academic work into limbo, my training as a historian has been put to good use in researching and writing this account.

Becoming an owner of the resort brought with it a much more acute appreciation of the perils and trials of business in general and ski resort operations in particular. I acquired a respect for the businessmen in Collingwood and the surrounding area. Their activities seem to be in the front line of the battle to provide jobs and a decent standard of living for the community. They are usually the leaders in many community endeavours and the first to be called upon when a new arena or hospital is required. They are frequently the target of various discontents, beleaguered by government inspectors and tax collectors, and oppressed by an increasing tide of paperwork and regulations. The ski resort operator has all these trials and more. The shortness of the season forces him to squeeze maximum efficiency from his operation, and he is as exposed to the whims of nature as the Saskatchewan farmer whose fields are suddenly turned into dust by drought or eaten by locusts.

Our resort enjoys more security than in the days of Jozo, thanks in part to his unflagging efforts. He was a multi-talented businessman, the likes of which are seldom found in this age of specialization. One of his most astonishing feats was the founding and developing of a pottery business that saved his ski resort operation. Another strength was the personal attention that he paid to his employees and customers. Seldom would a day go by when an employee did not see him or talk with him. His parties made him a legend with Blue Mountain skiers and guests, who drank his mulled wine served from a kettle at the "Sugar Shack" at the South Chair. On Mondays he would make the rounds in Collingwood hospital, visiting skiers who ended up there with broken legs and other injuries. While it is difficult to maintain this kind of personal contact in a large-scale operation like Blue Mountain today, "management by walking about" coninues to be important. It is to be hoped that respect for our employees and attentiveness to our customers will be one of Jozo's permanent legacies to Blue Mountain.

As I write this book, the face of Blue Mountain and the lands of Craigleith below the mountain are being reshaped by a tide of construction, some of it launched by our company and some of it by newly arrived developers. Monuments of the past are being obliterated. My earliest childhood memory is from the fall of 1941 when I was getting in the way of my father and his workmen, who were frantically hammering down the flooring of Blue Mountain Lodge, which was scheduled to open for the winter of that year. The Lodge is no longer there, swept away to make room for a modern condominium hotel. Blue Mountain's own bulldozers have destroyed the Ski Barn and other old buildings around the resort.

Along with my father, some of the personalities in my narrative have been removed by death. No longer with us is Ernie McCulloch, whose elegant skiing graced the slopes of Tremblant and Blue Mountain for many a decade. He was capable of doing 30 kilometres of cross-country skiing a day and could have gone on many years but for the cancer that ravaged him. The relatively short life of the flamboyant chalet owner and *bon vivant* Ted Henerofsky was recently remembered and celebrated by his friends at the Toronto Ski Club. Also gone from the scene are the artists Walter Trier and Robert Kemp. Kemp's Artist's Studio was destroyed by fire, and the surrounding original chalets are being torn down and replaced by more elaborate homes.

The majority of the ski pioneers are still here, however, and their presence is strongly felt. Many of them are still skiing, utilizing Blue Mountain's free season pass for those older than 65. When I talk to them or read their letters I find it is easy to be nostalgic in thinking about the ski trains, the sleigh tow and the Ski Barn. They were monuments of an era when pleasures were simpler and cheaper, and people did more to entertain themselves rather than depending on complex amusements delivered by technology. Of the successive generations that I have described, it is the generation that skied here in the Forties that I find the most interesting and attractive. These were men and women who experienced the joys of discovering untracked logging trails and powder, started ski resorts, rode wacky contraptions like the Red Devil, shouldered their skis and rucksacks at the Craigleith train station and trudged up the hill toward Blue Mountain Lodge. In addition, many of them participated in a great adventure that those of my generation can only read about in books or hear about second-hand around the fireplace. Thinking about my friend Ross Wilson, ski jumper, corvette commander and founder of ski resorts, I try to imagine his experience in a great episode of human history. He was there at the centre of the action in a smoke-filled line of warships and thundering gunfire. In contrast, my contemporaries and I have lived our lives in peaceful circumstances. My own children have lived a yet more secure and comfortable youth at the foot of Blue Mountain.

I feel fortunate in that I am old enough to have known some of the men and women of the Forties when they were in their prime and to have had a taste of their experiences. I accompanied my father when he met skiers disembarking from the trains in our army truck, and sometimes we rode on the train to Collingwood from Craigleith. I rode the Red Devil and mastered my fear of the "S" turns on the Dieppe downhill. I was part of a crew led by Orm Lougheed and Gordon Campbell that cut the new trails to accompany the pomalift that replaced the Red Devil. We used axes and crosscut saws to fell the trees and a team of horses to draw them out. I helped dig by hand the holes for the lift towers on our first chairlift at the south. Chain saws, bulldozers and ready-mix concrete trucks were soon to be introduced, making our earlier methods seem obsolete and ridiculously difficult. Craigleith was a farming community whose demise took place gradually before my eyes. At the neighbouring Goodchild farm I participated in a communal threshing, which was an enjoyable village ritual of sorts and was probably the last such event in these parts. The men worked frantically, throwing sheaves around in the dust-filled barn, while the women prepared a feast of meat, potatoes and home-baked pies.

Ski competitions were not as deadly serious as they are today. The cult of the amateur prevailed. It was not good form to train too hard or to wear a helmet in downhills. In the 1950s many of us competed in both Alpine and Nordic events. For a weekend competition we would load up our slalom skis, a pair of downhill skis for those who could afford them, the wide heavy jumping skis with three grooves for stability and the skinny wooden cross-country skis that had to be prepped elaborately with a torched-on pine-tar base. There would be downhill and slalom on a Saturday, a 15- or 20-kilometre cross-country race on Sunday morning, followed by jumping on a 50-metre hill in the afternoon, making for an exhausting but exhilarating weekend. This too was an era that soon passed, replaced by rigorous specialization in one, or at the most two, of the disciplines. Soon after my racing days, the *skimeister* or four-way skier became an extinct species. Our juniors here in Southern Ontario will not know, as we did in the 1950s, the frozen fear of staring out into space from the top of a jumping tower, the adrenalin rush of the takeoff and the joy of extending the body in flight.

Attractive as are some of the people and pursuits of the past, it would be wrong to ignore the benefits of new technology in the sport and to short-change newer generations. The recent band of racers led by Steve Podborski and Todd Brooker was hardly lacking in discipline and mettle. In terms of international significance, their achievements eclipsed those of previous Ontario ski racers.

Those who are elderly or middle-aged are quick to criticize the self-indulgence and near decadence of the yuppie generation, epitomized by the blazing designer ski suits and rock bands in the base lodges. While the younger generation of skiers does appear pampered in contrast to the old, there has always been a strong interest in fashions, and après-ski enjoyment of various kinds was always part of the sport. The charms of the total skiing and after-skiing experience are perhaps even more important today in providing relief and escape from the harrowing pressures of modern careerism and urban living.

The early facilities were charming and quaint, but it was a tedious thing to wait in line for the Red Devil or to climb half an hour up to the top of the hill for a run that lasted only two or three minutes. It took 15 minutes to wrap long thongs around your boots, and your skis had to be taken off before getting on the sleigh. It was hard to get a comfortably fitting boot and the leather became wringing wet on mild days. Parkas and gloves were nowhere near as protective as those of today. Bear-trap bindings were unforgiving and caused hundreds of fractures. On one occasion I saw a 200-pound man break his leg so violently that he tore the bindings right out of the ski. Had he been equipped with modern safety toe and heel pieces he might not have been hurt or might only have twisted a knee or ankle. It was easy to rip out a steel edge on a rock or piece of bare ground, after which you would lose half a day waiting for your ski to be repaired. There was a lack of washrooms around the resort, and kitchen facilities would not have passed today's health regulations. The Blue Mountain Lodge and Ski Barn could have been fatal places to be in the event of fire. The Lodge's fire escape consisted of ropes that were to be thrown out the window and climbed down.

Until the early 1970s the most serious drawback, in the light of today's developments, was the absence of man-made snow. Mild weather could bring a heart-breaking Chinese water torture to the resort operator and his employees. The rain always seemed to come just before the weekends. It would wash away the snow while my father stood helplessly by after having provisioned his kitchens and ordered in his staff, anticipating a major crowd. Many of our Christmas holidays were wiped out by mild weather. On one of them my sister and I had nothing to do but play canasta for 14 days straight. (I became so sick of card games that I have hated them ever since.) There were other winters which were very cold but snowless, excellent for skating on frozen ponds but infuriating for my father, who was powerless until somewhat supported by the rudimentary snowmaking system that he installed at the end of the 1960s.

In the 1950s conditions at the resort were not announced by electronic signs like the ones we have today. Instead there was a large blackboard, which Jozo would inscribe each weekend. On one Christmas Day he was delighted by a sudden fall of nearly a foot of snow. "Conditions Excellent," he jubilantly wrote. During the following night – a Friday night before what would have been a busy weekend – the temperature suddenly shot up and a downpour of rain washed the new snow completely away. Jozo erased the "Conditions Excellent" notation and replaced it with "The Lord hath given and the Lord hath taken away." Today, as a result of Blue Mountain's mammoth man-made snow production, a family can safely plan on a winter's skiing with minimal interruptions. The high-capacity lifts allow the company to make maximum use of Ontario's relatively short winter season. Inventions such as the slide rides and summer sports, golf, tennis and board sailing allow strong year-round operations and greater employment opportunities. The jobs provided by recreational and tourist operations and by chalet and condominium construction have replaced many of those lost by the decline of the rust-belt industries in Collingwood.

In the early 1980s I headed a committee of interested citizens who lobbied the Ontario government to restore the ski trains. While I regret that our effort failed, there is comfort in the fact that the railway line is being put to good use by the construction of the Georgian Trail.

The advent of ski operations on the mountain did not cause the decline of the farming community, as the land in these parts was poor and the farms were already in difficulty. Young people in Craigleith and Collingwood have a better chance today of remaining in their community because of the wider range of career opportunities.

Jozo's hope that Ontarians would learn to love winter and use Blue Mountain as their playground has been realized by the large numbers of skiers and recreationists who have chosen to frequent the resort and build year-round retreats for vacationing or to settle here for the remainder of their lives. The Blue Mountain and Collingwood community is a wonderful place in which to live. Barbara and I have ended up back here after a rather circular journey. She uncomplainingly followed me from the sunlit campus of Berkeley, California, where we met and married, to the frozen city of Moscow, where I spent almost a year studying Russian history; then it was on to the bleak suburbs of Downsview when I got my teaching job at York, and from there to Blue Mountain. She has flourished here, having become a dynamo in promoting theatre and the arts, and pursuing her economic development work in the Georgian Triangle. I dedicate this book to her. Our two children, who could ski to the Big Baby lift from our chalet – the one built by Jozo – have had an idyllic life at the foot of the mountain. They are at university now.

My sister Helen, with whom I grew up at the home farm and around the Ski Barn in the 1950s, has raised a family and is very happily married to Don McGillivray, whom she met when he was a ski patroller here 30 years ago. They live in Toronto but have a chalet in the Pretty River Valley, on a beautiful property originally owned by our parents. Jozo bought it because of its sparkling clear stream, which gave him the idea of starting a water-bottling company there, a project that he never got around to. Once again he was ahead of his time; water bottling is now a thriving business. For years Helen was unable to set foot on a pair of skis because of a painful back problem, but last winter she was miraculously feeling better and was again attacking a slalom course, this time with the Blue Mountain team in the Todd Brooker Challenge. Her son Jamie recently graduated from the Cornell University School of Hotel Administration and has taken a position in Banff. There is now at least one member of the third generation who is trained in the hospitality field.

The Collingwood-born twins who, like their older sister, enjoyed glorious ski victories in their youth, have been living in the area since Jozo's death. Katherine Canning lives with her husband, Gordon, in a house they built in the Apple Orchard overlooking Georgian Bay. Their daughter, Andrea, is an accomplished ski racer; she completed one year at the National Ski Academy and is now in her final year in Collingwood High School. Anna married a Czechoslovak, Joseph Marik, and lives with her family in our former farmhouse. Her son and daughter are the only grandchildren of Jozo and Helen who can speak our family's original language.

My mother has returned to the area after a long absence. Her hardy constitution allowed her to survive the shock of immigration, the rigours of homesteading in the Peace River District, and the severe hardships of starting the resort and pottery businesses at Blue Mountain. But she was devastated by the sudden loss of Jozo and needed to get away for a time. She removed herself to the south coast of Spain, learned Spanish, wrote poetry and built a new life that she led for 15 years among the simple people of a small Andalusian village. The Spanish interlude was wrapped up by a literary effort, a long narrative poem about her life. She called it *Mountain Ballad*. Last year she returned to be with her family and live in a chalet that we built for her near the bottom of the Apple Bowl.

The one whom we are without is, of course, Jozo. The death of such a larger-than-life personality creates a yawning hole that can never be filled. It has been a solace, however, and I hope a contribution to the knowledge of the history of the area, to record his achievements and those of his successors.

A winter rainbow of colours.

– Courtesy: Blue Mountain Resorts Limited, Credit: Henry Georgi

Descending Hog's Back. – Courtesy: Blue Mountain Resorts Limited, Credit: Henry Georgi

The cutting edge. – Courtesy: Blue Mountain Resorts Limited, Credit: Henry Georgi

Pretty in pink. – Courtesy: Blue Mountain Resorts Limited

Life on Easy Street. – Courtesy: Blue Mountain Resorts Limited, Credit: John de Visser

Look who dropped in on Carnival Day! – Courtesy: Blue Mountain Resorts Limited

Slipper Dipping. – Courtesy: Blue Mountain Resorts Limited

Love in the air. – Courtesy: Blue Mountain Resorts Limited, Credit: Henry Georgi

Condominium living at Blue Mountain.
– Courtesy: Blue Mountain Resorts Limited, Credit: Henry Georgi

Indian Summer. – Courtesy: Blue Mountain Resorts Limited, Credit: Dan McCracken

An impromptu picnic. – Courtesy: Blue Mountain Resorts Limited

Fireside kids. – Courtesy: Blue Mountain Resorts Limited, Credit: Michael Odesse

Early morning workout.
– Courtesy: Blue Mountain Resorts Limited, Credit: C. Schembri

Gotcha! – Courtesy: Blue Mountain Resorts Limited, Credit: Henry Georgi

Jozo stirs the chili pot, 1970. – Courtesy: Blue Mountain Resorts Limited

A 1950 painting of the Blue Mountain Lodge by Walter Trier. Lodge guest Eleanor Hughes skis across to the Red Devil sleigh tow while two Weider children play with Topsy in the background.
– Courtesy: Mrs. Eleanor Hughes, Credit: Walter Trier

Overlooking Stagefright on Monterra. – Courtesy: Blue Mountain Resorts Limited, Credit: Mark Rich

Snowboarding has arrived.

– Courtesy: Blue Mountain Resorts Limited, Credit: John Kapusty

Team spirit.

– Courtesy: Blue Mountain Resorts Limited

Winter smiles.

– Courtesy: Blue Mountain Resorts Limited

Sunny solitude, Blue Mountain Peaks, 1985.
– Courtesy: Blue Mountain Resorts Limited

Tiny tykes. – Courtesy: Blue Mountain Resorts Limited, Credit: John de Visser

Powderhound!
– Courtesy: Blue Mountain Resorts Limited, Credit: Henry Georgi

The Pom-Pom pack. – Courtesy: Blue Mountain Resorts Limited

Fireside singsong. – Courtesy: Blue Mountain Resorts Limited

Walter Trier created this cover for Blue Mountain's 1949-50 brochure depicting the activity around the north end, Gatehouse and Blue Mountain Lodge. – Courtesy: Mrs. Madeleine Harvie, Credit: Walter Trier

Happy sliders. – Courtesy: Blue Mountain Resorts Limited

Blue Mountain's Slide Rides.
– Courtesy: Blue Mountain Resorts Limited, Credit: Mark Rich

Shooting the Tube. – Courtesy: Blue Mountain Resorts Limited

Blowing up a storm.

– Courtesy: Blue Mountain Resorts Limited, Credit: C. Schembri

Night vision.

– Courtesy: Blue Mountain Resorts Limited

Dome at dawn.

– Courtesy: Blue Mountain Resorts Limited, Credit: John de Visser

The Silver Bullet. – Courtesy: Blue Mountain Resorts Limited, Credit: Henry Georgi

One of the many Trier cows that presided in the Ski Barn. "Applebowl Snowflake Lived Here 1898 till 1907 A.D. Double Granddaughter out of dam Powdersnow-Beauty. R.O.P., R.J.J.," c. 1951.
– Courtesy: Anna Marik, Credit: Walter Trier

Making tracks. – Courtesy: Blue Mountain Resorts Limited, Credit: Henry Georgi

Georgian Bay sunset. – Courtesy: Blue Mountain Resorts Limited

Mountain night life.

– Courtesy: Blue Mountain Resorts Limited, Credit: Henry Georgi

A Blue panorama. – Courtesy: Blue Mountain Resorts Limited

Jozo's family, Christmas 1989.
– Courtesy: Blue Mountain Resorts Limited, Credit: Steve Montgomery

Left to right, front row: *Relationship to Jozo Weider. Tony Marik, Grandson; Gillian McGillivray, Granddaughter; Joseph Marik, Son-In-Law; Katherine Weider, Granddaughter; Helen Weider, Wife; Andrea Canning, Granddaughter; Gordon Canning, Son-In-Law; Left to right, back row: Katherine Canning, Daughter; Michael Weider, Grandson; Jamie McGillivray, Grandson; Helen McGillivray, Daughter; Alec McGillivray, Grandson; Anna Marik, Daughter; Don McGillivray, Son-In-Law; Tessa Marik, Granddaughter; Barbara Weider, Daughter-In-Law; George Weider, Son.*

Acknowledgements

Abbotts, Harold
Art Gallery of Ontario
Belcher, Mike
Beedell, Mike
Blair, Bob
Blue Mountain Resorts Limited
Boehm, Sue
Bowie, Doug
Brooker, Chuck & Joyce
Brooker, Todd
Brydon, Bert
Butler, Al
Canadian National Railways
Canadian Ski Museum
Canning, Gordon & Katherine
Carruthers, Doug
Casey, Kellie
Champagne, Ed
Chapman, Herb
Charlton, Bob & Mary Ellen
Clark, Burny
Cochran, David
Collingwood *Enterprise-Bulletin*
Collingwood Library
Collingwood Museum
Collingwood Ski Club
Colombo, John Robert
Crews, Diane
Crossan, Bob & Ilene
Crysler, Eileen
Cummings, Gord
Czerny, Doug
Czerny, George
Deacon, D.O.
De Visser, John
Dunbar, Elizabeth "Ebie" Snively
Durnford, Philip
Eagleson, R. Alan
Egnal, Marc
Fodor, Gretl
Garrad, Charles
Gee, Michael
Georgas, Bill
Georgas, Jim
Georgio, Henry
Gillespie, Ian
Glaysher, Brian & Shirley
Gooch, Bob
Goodchild, John
Gordon, Bev Beecham
Granatstein, Jack
Griffith, Ottilie Galbraith
Forsythe, Ruth
Fujino, Paul & Mary
Hall, Herb
Harrison, Mr. & Mrs. Ted
Harvie, Mrs. Madeleine
Hiegelsberger, Rudy
Hughes, Mrs. Eleanor
Hughes, Paul
Jaroch, Mike & Mary
Jessop, George J.
Kamps, Leslie
Keith, Marcella Plater
Kemp, Barb
Kerschbaumer, Bob
Kilgour, Mrs. Mary
Kimble, Helen
Kingsmill, Allison
Kingsmill, Peter
Knott, Bill
Lailey, Mr. & Mrs. T. B.
Langmuir, Pat
Larway, Ross
Layhew, Gord
LeGrice, Madge
Lorne, Bob
MacInnis, Jeff
MacMurchy, Ian
MacMurchy, Jack
Marsh, Tracy
Marik, Joseph & Anna
Martinek, Joe & Brenda
McCracken, Dan
McDonald, Ted
McGillivray, Helen
McGuire, Tom
McKendrick, Bunny
McNichol, Dale
McNichol, Dave
McNulty, Frank
McVicar, Alex
Metras, Shiela
Miller, Ken
Montgomery, Steve
National Alpine Ski Team
National Ski Academy
Owen Sound *Sun-Times*
Paul, Dr. Don
Perry, Peter
Philp, Bev
Plater, Donald
Plater, Larry
Podborski, Jackie
Ponton, Alex & Rusty
Rich, Mark
Richardson, Mrs. Mary
Robertson, Stewart
Rogers, Ian
Rowland, Jim & Lisa
Saunders, Dave
Saunders, Jack
Schembri, C.
Schuller Fotography
Schuller, Fritz
Sheffer, Joe
Sheridan, Aubrey & Lois
Sheridan, Ron & Imogene
Skelton, Bill & Sue
Skelton, Ken
Somborac, Milan & Judith
Stephenson, Lee
Thomas, Marijane
Tindale, Bill
Toronto Ski Club
Town of Collingwood
Township of Collingwood
Trier, Mrs. Walter
Trusler, Connie Sparrow
Tucker, Les
University of Toronto Archive
Wallace, Doug & Katie
Ward-Price, Wendy
Warll, Lynn
Weider, Barbara
Weider, Mrs. Helen
Westlake, Audrey
Wieland, Hans
Williams, Joe
Wilson, Ross
Yates, Art & Pat
Zotter, Karl

Bibliography

Arp, Barbara, ed. *Reflections—Collingwood: An Historical Anthology* Elmvale, Ontario: Bayweb Press, 1983.

Art Gallery of Ontario. *Humorist Walter Trier: Selections From The Trier-Fodor Foundation Gift.* Toronto, Ontario: Gilchrist-Wright Limited, 1980.

Ball, W. L. *I Skied the Thirties.* Ottawa, Ontario: Deneau Publishers & Company Ltd., 1979.

Carmichael, W.J. *Sports Personalities of Collingwood.* Collingwood, Ontario: McNulty Printing, 1983.

Douglas, H. Percy. *My Ski-ing Years.* Montreal, Quebec: Whitcombe & Gilmour Limited, 1951.

Hall, Fred, ed. *Fifty Years of Skiing in Southern Ontario with the Toronto Ski Club.* Inter-Collegiate Press of Canada (1971) Ltd., 1974.

Main, Mollie. *Craigleith Ski Club.* Collingwood, Ontario: Bennett Press, 1978.

McCulloch, Ernie. *Ski Easy . . . The New Technique.* Montreal, Quebec: McGraw-Hill Ryerson Limited, 1973.

Podborski, Steve. *Podborski.* Toronto, Ontario: McClelland and Stewart, 1987.

Shannon, Bill. *An Illustrated History of Collingwood Township.* Craigleith, Ontario: Bennett Press, 1979.

Index

Trail Map

Lifts

Chairlifts

A Big Baby Triple
B O-Hill Double
C South Double
D L-Hill Triple
E Tranquility Double
F Apple Bowl Double
G Inn Triple
H Spectacular Double
I North Double
J Easy Street Beginner

Rope Tow

K North Rope

Poma Lifts

L North
M Apple Bowl
N Big Baby

Skiing

- 27 trails (6 trails night skiing)
- 720' (219.4 m) vertical
- longest run 4,000' (1,219 m)
- 96% snowmaking coverage

Accommodation

- Blue Mountain Inn
- Chateau Ridge Condominiums
- Cachet Crossing Condominiums
- Wintergreen Condominiums

South Base Lodge

- licensed cafeteria
- licensed lounge
- fast food
- ski shop
- rental shop
- ski school
- restrooms
- pay phones
- tickets

Trails of the 1990s.